ADDITIONAL PRAISE FOR
Uppity Women of the Renaissance

"I've been a fan of Vicki León's Uppity Women from the moment I started reading her *Uppity Women of Medieval Times.* I love her witty style and attention to detail, and her ability to make these somewhat forgotten women come alive in only a few words. Her newest book, *Uppity Women of the Renaissance,* delivers the same fun, quality experience I've come to expect. Vicki's short, humorous windows into the lives of these remarkable women provide a starting point for exploration, and ensure that they will not be forgotten again. Bravo, Vicki!"

> —*Colleen Bell,* Library Instruction Coordinator,
> University of Oregon

"Vicki León continues her wonderfully flippant 'world herstory' with *Uppity Women of the Renaissance,* introducing us to a multitude of interesting ladies hitherto unfairly overlooked. An informative read that is also fun."

> —*Barbara G. Walker,* author of *Feminist Fairy Tales, The Woman's*
> *Encyclopedia of Myths and Secrets, The Crone, Women's Rituals,* and
> *The Woman's Dictionary of Symbols and Sacred Objects*

"Sometimes feminist scholarship takes itself too seriously. Vicki León's *Uppity Women* series is a great antidote. This latest venture is a lighthearted peek at the behind-the-curtain-of-history doings of an amazing array of Renaissance women from printer-publishers, peddlars, and poisoners, through soldiers, sheriffs, and thieves, to nuns and queens. How has Vicki found them all? Lots of food for reflection here."

> —*Elise Boulding*, professor emeritus of sociology,
> Dartmouth College, and author of *Underside of History*

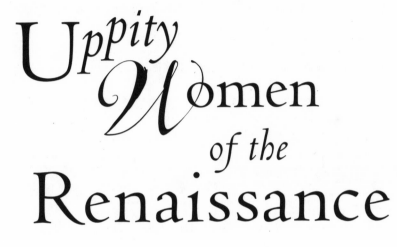

Uppity Women of the Renaissance

VICKI LEÓN

CONARI PRESS
Berkeley, California

The Brideling, Sadling, and Ryding of a rich Churle in Hampshire, London 1595, courtesy of The Huntington Library, San Marino, Calfornia.

Woodcut: interior of l'Hôtel Dieu, courtesy of Giraudon/Art Resource, New York.

Portrait of Aphra Amis Behn by Peter Lely, courtesy of The Library of Congress.

Virgin and Child by Fra Filippo Lippi, courtesy of Alinari/Art Resource, New York.

Cover illutration: *Le Tricheur à l'As de Carreau* by Georges de La Tour (detail)
Cover and book design: Claudia Smelser

Library of Congress Cataloging-in-Publication Data

León, Vicki
    Uppity Women of the Renaissance / by Vicki León.
        p.   cm.
    Includes bibliographical reference and index.
    ISBN: 1-57324-127-X
    1. Women–History–Renaissance. 1350–1650.
    2. Women–Europe–Biography. 3. Renaissance. I. Title.
HQ1148.L46 1999
305.4'092'24–dc21   98–43618
                                        CIP

Printed in the United States of America on recycled paper
Conari Press books are distributed by Publishers Group West.

00 01 02 03 DR 10 9 8 7 6 5 4 3

To Robert Stanard Thompson, the best friend
and colleague an uppity woman could have

and

to the amazing staff of the Ocean Park Washington Library and the Timberland
Regional Library system, without whose help, hair-trigger response time, and
unfailing good cheer this book would not have become a reality.

UPPITY WOMEN
OF THE RENAISSANCE

Born Again—But to What?	I
Crafty Women & Artful Iron Maidens	9
Disorderly Dames, Ardent Altruists & Law-and-Order Ladies	49
Brilliant Blue Collars, Soulful Femmes & Yuppies of Yore	9I
Rolling Stones & Gender-Adventurous Gals	127
Slick Talkers & Awesome Networkers	163
Career Virgins, Saintly Souls & Wa-a-ayward Women	197
The Mrs., Misses & Near Misses of King Henry VIII	235
Better Halves, Daring Daughters & Significant Others of the Rich & Famous	257
Renaissance Resources	295
Selected Bibliography	30I
Index of Uppity Women	304

BORN AGAIN—
BUT TO WHAT?

From grade school on, we've had it dinned into our ears that *renaissance* meant "rebirth." But rebirth into what? And just who got reborn, come to think of it?

Beginning around the mid-1300s, a change occurred in the way that people throughout Europe thought. Prior to that time, nine out of ten Europeans believed that laws (and everything else) were made by a higher power. God was a law-and-order deity, and the Catholic Church was his SWAT team.

Then some iconoclastic fellow or damsel got a bizarre notion. What would the world be like if, say, *individuals* were important? What if you could open your horizons to the literature, art, and moral philosophy of the classical past, and the scientific inquiry of the future, while still keeping on the good side of that celestial J. Edgar Hoover?

It sounds kooky, I know. But by degrees, this crazy idea, called "humanism," caught hold. Then glamour geeks like fifteenth-century Dutch satirist Desiderius Erasmus proclaimed, "Hey! I'm a humanist."

By his day, female humanists were already coming out of the woodwork. Learned and lippy Italians like the Nogarola sisters, Laura Cereta, Cassandra Fedele, and Olimpia Morata got famous swapping zingers with male humanists. In England, later thinkers like Bathsua Makin, the Cooke sisters, and three out of the six wives of Henry

I

VIII spread the idea, while French intellectuals like alchemist and much-in-demand speaker Marie le Jars got into the act.

Once celebrities were on board, it wasn't long before the media ran with it, goosed by the fortuitous arrival of printing from metal type in the 1450s. The advent of quick copies created a flood of books and pamphlets on humanism and other hot new topics. Soon printing and publishing pioneers from Charlotte Guillard to Hester Ogden were cranking out publications with their male competitors—and they weren't all recipe books or religious tomes, either. A mere fifty years after Gutenberg, 12 million books were in print, most at prices even within the reach of a sorely strapped housewife. By now, a whole lot of folks were reading. In a trice, maybe two, readers became independent thinkers.

Your average European wench in the street started muttering: "Hmm, this humanism thing. Sure, it's a shot in the dark, but just speaking hypothetically . . . what if *women* were individuals too?" When *that* one hit the fan, a collective shudder went through popes, bishops, kings, and other affiliates of organized religion.

"More funding for inquisitions," came the call. (Better to be safe than sorry, when keeping women in their place.) Economies all over Europe perked up, thanks to healthy infusions of cash and manpower from the office of inquisitions and general prying. Despite their truly diabolical efforts at witch-

Hmm—is this what they mean by humanism?

hunting, Jew persecuting, and heretic harassing, it was too late. Individualism was out of the bag. Along with peasants, Jews, gypsies, and other downtrodden, underreported, underpaid segments of European society, women wanted their own rebirth. (By this time, they'd certainly had their anesthetic-free fill of *birthing*.)

Although books spread good ideas, they also spread bad ones. A toxic best-seller called the *Witches' Hammer*, published in 1486, quickly found its way onto the desk of every bureaucrat, religious official, and misogynist nut case in Europe. Written by a pair of prestigious but deeply disturbed priests, the *Hammer's* pages gave a rationale for persecuting women and a how-to for hunting them down. Even worse, its "facts" soon oozed into civil law. Besides demonizing an entire gender as "the insatiable sex most likely to have intercourse with the devil," the book gave helpful hints for finding generic "witches' marks" on the body of any socially indigestible (read: independent or vocal) female. No social classes were safe—even altruistic queens like Joan of Navarre got jailed sans trial. Although more than 100,000 women were ultimately tortured and executed during the hottest centuries (1500 to 1700), some escaped thanks to their support networks—like Ursula Fladin, whose family formed a collective to Sherlock her case.

By Martin Luther's day in the early 1500s, even the simplest soul, seeing the roaring business the Catholic Church did in peddling "get outta purgatory free" indulgences and the mistresses du jour of local

3

priests, thought the Mother Church was pretty corrupt. Protests erupted like teenage acne.

Soon a juicy crop of Protestant sects arose. As their first task, they immediately began warring with each other, as well as with Catholics. This in turn led to deadly dull (and just plain deadly) stretches of bellicosity. Though few could top the dreary Hundred Years' War (1337–1453) between the English and the French, the religious factions tried, with the Thirty Years' War (1618–1648), the English Civil War (1642–1649), and a variety of second-rate conflicts—you name 'em, men (and quite a few women) fought 'em.

To fill in the peace gaps, people compensated with local aggressions and wars against infidels, like the Turks. For instance, lands from England to Spain saw numerous riots led by women (sometimes in drag) over taxes, price controls, and agricultural issues. When English weaver Alice Clark captained a mob of rioting weavers in 1629, the event was voted the year's best protest—especially after she got the male weavers to don dresses as well.

Given gunpowder and the more lethal weapons used in warfare, plus plagues, sweating sickness, and other high-mortality developments, Europe's population shrank to a tidy sixty million or so by 1500. In places like Germany, despite the ghastly toll taken by childbearing, women outnumbered men. With the discovery of several new continents that called out for exploitation, to say nothing of all the deferred maintenance awaiting after centuries of plague, there was even more work to be done than in prior centuries.

Unfortunately, there didn't appear to be nearly enough jobs. People blamed it on comets, conflicts, the weakening of the guilds, the breakdown of the social order. Part of the problem was simple lack of currency. At times, pepper and sugar had to serve for debt payment. The lust for metals to make more coinage opened a few earthy opportunities for women—although schlepping ore was a rough way to make your daily bread (and good luck cashing those sugar paychecks).

Even without prosperity, women stepped up to become sheriffs and goldsmiths, carpenters and barber-surgeons. As *femmes soles* or indie businesswomen, they made demands. And money. Dorothy Petty cleaned up in the insurance game; Joan Dant, with underwear; Karyssa Under Helmslegern, with copper; and Eulalia Sagarra, with soap. Feminine risk takers like Benvenida Abravanel and Bess of Hardwick took up money lending or international trade, or became spokeswomen for new religious movements, like Quaker Margaret Fell and First Lady Lutheran Katie von Bora. As in prior centuries, females were in the forefront of fledgling religious sects, and made maximum use of their opportunities, money, and clout.

Although they weren't what they had been, guilds (the early equivalent of unions) still functioned. European women paid their dues as silk workers or metalsmiths, fishmongers or glovers, to get in on group insurance, take part in annual feasts to patron saints, and wear the garb (or "livery" as it was called) of their guild.

Women had to weather other Renaissance horrors—the Great Schism, for one. Besides being difficult to spell, the Great Schism split the audience for the Supreme Pontiff by setting up rival pope shops in Avignon, France, and Rome. However, most people considered the *real* schism to be a fashion issue, caused by uppity women.

The ruffians who ran the rival papacies (1378–1417) made love as often as they made war on each other. Entranced by a gold-digging Goldilocks or two, they began a "popes prefer blondes" campaign. This quickly led to a revolution among high-end hookers, who began bleaching their long tresses.

By now your average woman of respectability clamored for the same sun-kissed appearance, leading to a run on eggshells, alum, orange peel, and other materials thought to have peroxide powers. Explorers tackled uncharted seas and lands in a desperate search to find industrial quantities of goat dung and sulfur.

But hair wasn't the only thing being changed. In an effort to get fewer women in the workplace and more women-in-their-place, male movers and shakers turned to the time-honored "Pregnancy is bliss" idea. Artists began to feature big-bellied women in every picture. After they stopped laughing, Ren women enthusiastically adopted the padded "bustin' out all over" look—a faux pregnancy fashion statement that deeply puzzled later generations. (Once a Mrs. discovered that her dress would let her pass for pregnant, the garments became de facto birth control devices.)

At the same time women were putting it all out front, so were men. To set off his skin-tight hose and padded jackets, the fashionable male sported a codpiece, a jeweled and sequined "Lookie here!" cup that just screamed self-esteem. Or something. Sex ed classes for women became superfluous; they were surrounded by men in tights, whose buns and other body parts could be studied at leisure.

Interestingly, the typical male getup of the period (long hair, gussied-up hats, flowing garments with lots of ribbons, tights), made it easier for women to pass as young males. Instead of "I wanna be me!" a growing number of females barked, "I wanna be male!"

Cross-dressing had pragmatism going for it. In England, from 1660 on, actresses had ample chance to wear the pants; nearly 25 percent of all plays produced had breeches roles. But job opportunities were most plentiful in the military, from soldier and sailor to rent-a-mercenary. The caloric benefits alone made such a life attractive, especially to a damsel in dire straits who didn't care to sell herself. Other gals cross-dressed to experiment with a gender that looked to be more fun, or to stalk a loved one in the service.

Frequently, however, women found that cross-dressing was a slick way to live outside the law. Especially during the sixteenth and seventeenth centuries, a number of scalawags, including German arsonist Isabella Geelvinck, Dutch annuity scammer Cornelia Croon, and French duelist and theater

Mom in labor?
Nope—it's the "Renaissance is bustin' out all over" fashion statement.

7

darling Aubigny de Maupin, adorned wanted posters and confused law enforcement. Europeans had a fascination for gender-adventurous women. Battle heroines like Trijntje Simon and lovable rascals like Long Meg became the subject of popular songs and ballads—the lyrics of which were printed in mass market quantities and sold in huge numbers.

So, you ask, why did so many of these rip-roaring Renaissance women, reborn to raise Cain or raise consciousness, vanish from our view? One clue might lie in surnames. During these centuries, surnames—the more, the murkier—spread like wildfire. Among those with upwardly mobile pretensions, the idea was to have a name as long as the train of your dress. The side effect of that thicket of aliases, however, was to render many a woman invisible—even to her immediate ancestors.

More than once, today's scholars have posed the question: "Did women in Europe even *have* a Renaissance?" These scholars have a point. During Ren times, women lost ground they'd gained in legal rights and education, got pushed out of careers they'd previously participated in, and suffered through a centuries-long female-hating holocaust. To my mind, that just makes the long litany of proud and passionate women you're going to read about deserve even more attention and praise. To achieve rebirth in good times is dandy; but to triumph in tough times, as did the more than two hundred redoubtable females profiled here, was frankly and fantastically uppity.

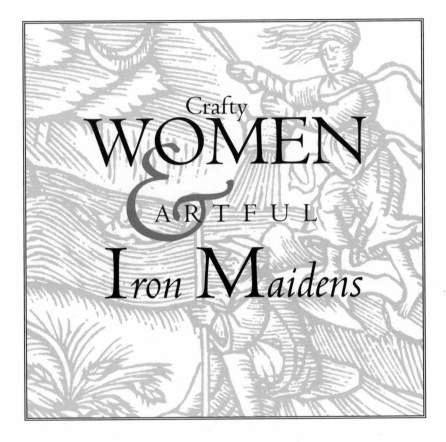

Crafty
WOMEN
&
ARTFUL
Iron Maidens

AGGRAVATED ASSAULT WITH
A DAIRY PRODUCT

ot all accused witches stood alone—and not all witch-hunts had a fiery ending, fortunately. Take the case of **Ursula Fladin,** a woman in her sixties from the village of Durrenthal in Saxony.

In 1581, Ursula got hit with a sorcery charge. One man claimed Mrs. Fladin had "given him diarrhea"; a second asserted she'd harmed his cattle five years earlier. A third charge came from a dead man, said to have gotten ill after stealing milk from Ursula. The final accusation came from pastor Martin Heintz, who'd found a "pipe or reed, sweaty and dripping with cream," stuck in a skull in the church graveyard.

Ursula said it was bushwah. "I did do the reed and cream thing," she conceded, "but only to find out who'd stolen my milk." Predictably, no one cared about *her* milk thievery.

Mrs. Fladin was locked up and questioned under torture. By now, her husband and scandalized family had lodged a formal protest against the judge and were doing their own Sherlock work on the charges. Most of the "evidence" crumbled. The pastor, for instance, had heard about the sweating reed from Ursula herself in confession! (So much for the sanctity of the confessional booth.)

After fifteen weeks and a day, Ursula got released. She'd been tortured enough to cripple one arm and make her permanently lame.

Still, the family got a nice warm Colombo feeling at having gotten her out. After her "You've been sprung!" party, they slapped a suit against the judge for wrongful arrest, imprisonment, and torture—plus compensation of thirty shillings for each day of imprisonment.

Meanwhile, that dratted pastor popped up again, complaining to the authorities about Ursula's "godless behavior." Since he'd accused her of sorcery, Mrs. Fladin had refused to go to his services but still wanted Holy Communion—can you believe it? Ursula was therefore ordered to attend pastor Heintz' church.

At the speed of a Saxony snail, the proceedings went forward. Since the lawyers defending the judge had such a lame case, they fell back on a Catch-22: They accused Ursula *again* of witchcraft, in order to get their client off on the charges of excessive and unjust torture! Then the judge's defense team got a series of adjournments reaching into the next year—by which time, a sorely tried Ursula Fladin had gone to meet her maker.

Her grimly determined heirs kept up the fight. The final court showdown was set for August 1587—a mere six years after the whole farce began. Unlike an episode of Colombo, history does not record what—if anything—was the ultimate verdict for Ursula.

I'm gonna beat this low-fat rap if it's the last thing I do!

MINERS, MONEY MANAGERS, & OTHER GOLD-FINGERERS

he Renaissance centuries are often called "golden"—a literal description, once the gold (and silver) from New World explorers started pouring into Spain and Portugal. Europe, on the other hand, had copper and silver mines, but mined most of its gold elsewhere. Much more than decorative objects upon which to drape 24-carat jewelry, women were involved in the entire mining and smithing process.

Take **Drutgin van Caster,** a German goldsmith who lived around 1500. She must have had real talent, for she became Artisan to the Emperor—that would be Emperor Maximilian, head of the Holy Roman Empire until 1519. Not all precious metal workers were so upstanding; in England, a certain **Oliva the Goldsmith** made various appearances in court, fined for breaking the Norwich trade regula-

Gold-sluicer, you idiot, not gold-digger!

tions. Guild records show there were a surprising number of female goldsmiths around Europe, especially in Nuremberg, Germany, which had a large labor force crafting finished gold products. Details on individuals are rare, though.

Women also labored to extract precious metals from the earth. Records—including pictorial art of women washing ore and schlepping baskets of it on their shoulders—show that mines in Saxony and elsewhere hired both sexes to do the heavy lifting. Women also made coins from ore. During the mid-1500s, in mining-rich Bohemia (today's Czech Republic), the most important mint in the country had a female CEO. Known as the "manager-mistress" of Kutna Hora, **Suzanne Erker** could rightly be called Bohemia's most outstanding money woman.

Ren daycare—give the kids a hammer.

13

BADGERED
BY PLAGUE

lthough the plague brought her medical mate plenty of business (albeit few repeat customers), **Mrs. Diogo Afonso** shared his dream to find a cure for the malady. For years, she put up with Diogo's weird experiments and disgusting smells in the basement of their Portuguese home.

Then he cooked up a cure that seemed sure-fire. "First you get a badger drunk," he told his wife, "on a wine mixed with gold, pearls, and coral, and filtered through some camphor. Then you behead the badger, drain its blood, and remove the organs." Stifling a retch, Mrs. Afonso watched him simmer the whole mess with spices (including a pinch of unicorn horn), until he had a compound that made up into a lovely powder.

Afonso's Plague-buster was a huge success around Portugal; after

a few years and some human trials, Diogo got rave testimonials from surviving patients. Pretty soon, King Duarte himself was a customer. Mr. and Mrs. Afonso were enjoying a good gloat when, darn it, she noticed that she'd come down with the plague as well.

The doctor ran to get a dose, tenderly administering it to his wife. Unfortunately, all he had on hand was a pinch of badger medication that had been on the shelf for a year or two—which, as any fool knew, went toxic on you.

Just before she expired in his arms, the long-suffering Mrs. Afonso said, "Diogo, quit badgering me!" But it was too late. Bad badger (and a nasty case of the plague) had struck again.

MAESTRAS
OF THE MOTET

taly, the land of the aria, was a congenial home for female composers. While dozens composed professionally, three got extraordinary recognition in Ren times: **Barbara Strozzi, Maddalana Casulana,** and **Tarquinia Molza.**

Adopted by a filthy rich banker of Venice, her mom a house servant, the possibly illegitimate Barbara got a head start in music from her musically talented dad Giulio. In the early 1600s, when she was barely twelve, Barbara had a singing gig with a musical group that met at the Strozzi mansion. She started composing in her twenties, publishing madrigals, motets, and arias. After her father died, this singular single went professional, composing for affluent patrons and performing her own compositions. Barbara's voice must have been exceptional; her compositions (over fifty still exist) were designed to showcase a lyrical soprano voice.

Born about 1540, singer Maddalena Messari Casulana wrote madrigals. In her forty-some years, she composed a three-volume collection of sixty-six madrigals—the first published by any woman. A sparkling and confident musician, Maddalena didn't think of herself as the exception to the rule. She once wrote to a patron: "I want to show the world the foolish error of men, who so greatly believe themselves to be the masters of high intellectual gifts that cannot, it seems to them, be equally common among women."

A third female composer of note—and notoriety—was Tarquinia Molza, who wrote for the harp, viol, lute, and voice, then conducted as well. She possessed a soprano as brilliant as Venetian glass. Italy and Europe could be a tough sell when it came to female voices; by the 1500s, the royal courts reserved their most fulsome kudos for the surgery-enhanced sopranos of male castrati singers. When Tarquinia came along in 1570 or so, her powerful voice cut through, if you'll pardon the expression, the castrati fad and stirred the public fancy. Established at the court of a duchess, her career *fortissimo,* Molza looked like a diva for the ages when disaster hit, in the form of a love affair with the wrong man. Exit Molza, *molto allegro.*

SAINT-INSPIRED SPORT

eave it to the Dutch to come up with a patron saint for skaters—not that **Lydwina of Schiedam** was any holiday on ice. One of nine kids from a good Catholic family, Lydwina from the time she toddled took a vow of chastity. As a teen, she prayed for a miracle: to become so ugly she'd never marry. Fate promptly obliged. In her iron skates, Lydwina took a tumble on the ice. Besides cracking a rib that broke through the skin and turned into a nasty permanent abscess, she hit her face. At length, to her joy, her facial wound grew into a huge oozing trench that ran from her forehead to her nose. Then this holy glutton for physical punishment threw on a horsehair girdle and spent the next thirty-eight years in bed, reveling in gangrene and from time to time, giving awed pilgrims a sample of her healing powers. In 1433, Holland's sight for sore eyes choked on her own phlegm and died, a feat that promptly gained her sainthood.

No doubt it was Saint Lydwina that **Judith Johannes** and **Marie Scholtus** prayed to when they set out to become star skaters in the seventeenth century. Every Dutch girl and woman lived on the ice. But few became celebrities like blade runners Judith and Marie. These two raced professionally, cheered on by huge noisy crowds that gathered along the canal banks of Amsterdam and other cities. In this affluent, dice-happy society, the Dutch gambled heavily on the outcomes of skating races, where pros like these two women (and others whose names have not survived) competed on a circuit all winter long.

Incidentally, the Dutch may have pioneered another sport on ice that they called "kolf." Judging by many Dutch paintings of the sixteenth and seventeenth centuries, it was commonly played on ice (and sometimes on grass) by women and even young girls. Kolf bore a decided likeness both to ice hockey and to a Scottish game played on a green by the likes of Mary, Queen of Scots—who, it's said, cleverly invented the concept of the caddie.

cherchez
la femme's logo

rtist **Judith Leyster** wanted to follow her star as a painter. Her name even spelled it out—*Leyster* means "lodestar" or guiding star in Dutch. When she signed a painting, Judith made a visual pun, adding a JL monogram and attaching a star to it.

Born in 1609 in Haarlem, Judith won wide acclaim in her own time—a reputation that went into eclipse at her marriage and by her death around 1668 had vanished almost completely. Funny. Just like many of her paintings. Centuries later, when *The Jolly Companions,* a work long chalked up to Dutch master Frans Hals, got cleaned, Judith's distinctive logo popped out. Since then, more Leyster works have been discovered (most of them long thought to be Hals' too).

Judging by her self-portrait at her easel, Judith had a confident air, an earthy exuberance for life that shines through her work. As a teen, she may have done apprenticeship in Utrecht. By 1629, she and her family moved back near Haarlem, where Judith joined the painters' guild, and probably became a student of Frans Hals. She would eventually have pupils of her own; three are known. She and Hals were even friends. For a while, that is; in 1635, however, she took her mentor to court on an ethics charge, and won. It seems Mr.

Hals had taken one of her former pupils as an apprentice—a guild no-no.

A painter of kaleidoscopic talents, Judith turned out portraits, still lifes, and genre paintings. As she matured creatively, the artist integrated social commentary about the inequality of male and female roles into her work.

Her most famous genre picture, *The Proposition,* shows a housewife bent over her sewing, being hit on by an old geezer, coins in hand: "Hey babe—why are you wasting your time on needlework when you could have a ball with me?" This painting contrasted sharply with countless works painted by male artists that showed a happy world of blowsy hookers and leering men—a *Hustler* view of life. With this work, Judith made a key contribution to art. She created a new iconography, one that related directly to her identity as a woman.

About 1636, Leyster's brewer dad went bankrupt. That same year, she married a vile-tempered wastrel of a painter named Jan Molenaer. Are these two events linked? It's suggestive. The couple moved to Amsterdam, where Judith struggled to paint. As children came along, she had her hands full—and more so, with Jan. An all-too-familiar face at court, he was twice convicted for brawling and other offenses. Despite his inheritance and their income as painters, Jan got deeply into debt. In trying to keep her family afloat, Judith's lodestar set prematurely. Only now is it rising to shine again.

A GREAT DANISH

er new husband, the king of Scotland, was no prize, thought fourteen-year-old **Anne of Denmark.** Phobic about assassins, the king wore padded clothes; as if his Scottish accent weren't enough, he had a speech impediment and tics, from head-twitching to constant eye-rolling. Still, he'd romantically come all the way to Norway to rescue his betrothed when Anne's ship had been pushed off course by a storm. (James was convinced that local witches could control prevailing winds and thus were trying to kill his bride-to-be via shipwreck.)

Some people get their sexual surprises on the wedding night— Anne, the first Dane to make queen of Scotland and later England, didn't get hers until after a six-month honeymoon. But it was a doozy. When the fulfilled (or so she thought) twosome arrived back in Edinburgh in 1590, James shyly confessed: "By the way, I'm a wee bit bisexual."

Wee wasn't the word. Over the years, this king had more famous flames than James Brown's band. His tolerant views on sexual partners notwithstanding, the king loved to persecute. He commissioned a King James version of the Bible, mistranslating a key phrase to read: "Thou shalt not suffer a witch to live!" That gave him free rein to carry out a huge number of the most vicious witch-hunts in Europe.

Meanwhile, Anne did her level best to produce heirs—not that easy when she had to coordinate conjugal visits with a long list of the king's "friends."

In 1603, she and James became rulers of England. Even at the coronation, the fur started to fly—this time over religion, not sex partners. Anne pooh-poohed the official Anglican Church of England, and refused to take Communion. She eventually became a full-fledged Catholic, much to James' chagrin.

Religious quarrels and sexual politics aside, Anne's greatest gift to her adoptive country was as a patron of the arts. She brought famed architect Inigo Jones to England and started a wave of building in the beautiful Jacobean style. This great Dane supported the arts and was particularly bountiful to Shakespeare, Ben Jonson, and other writers. At her court, Anne held masques (highly popular musical and dra-

It took a huffy woman to be a storm-brewer.

matic performances), taking part in some of them. This frivolity didn't draw much fire from the king, either. By this time, she and James had reached a separate but equal détente, their quarters diplomatically separated by a mere mile or two of drafty palace corridors.

SHE MADE MARSEILLES
A NO-WOMAN'S-LAND

f you've ever been lost in Marseilles, you may have run across the Boulevard des Dames. Ever wonder how it got its name? The women it honors were the die-hard troops of a "Go for it!" military miss named **Améliane de Glandèves.**

La Glandèves was just doing what came naturally. A loyal citizen of Marseilles, in 1524 she got caught in the cross fire of a petite civil war between the constable of Bourdon and the king of France. In a fit of testosterone madness, the constable thought that holding the port city of Marseilles hostage would be a good move to get the king's attention. So he laid siege to the place. The battle was getting ugly when reinforcements finally arrived for the locals. "*Sacre bleu,*" moaned the defenders. "It's a bunch of women!" Then: "*Mon Dieu—*their leader is the governor's daughter Améliane!"

Améliane evidently had quite a rep already as a battle-scarred vet. Without hesitation, she and her women warriors dove in, thrashing the constable's troops until they retreated.

A dirty tricks maestro, the constable said, "Okay, let's lay a bunch of mines and blow these women out of the water!"

But Améliane de Glandèves, herself a practitioner of the "All's fair in love and war" school, went the constable one further. She and her women got down in the dirt and dug another huge trench. In it, they planted their own mine field. What with mines and counter-mine fields, that part of Marseilles was a pretty dicey place to walk, I can assure you. To keep future generations from being blown derrière over teakettle, Améliane's explosive no-woman's-land became known as "Tranchée des Dames" or "the Women's Trench." When all the mines had exploded or become duds (or at least their "use by" date had expired), the Women's Trench became what it is today: the Women's Boulevard in downtown Marseilles.

In the siege's aftermath, a local fellow named Billy Puget simply swooned over Améliane's exploits, and asked her to marry him. When she agreed, he changed *his* name, proudly becoming Guillaume du Puget-Glandèves.

SPAIN'S GREATEST CHISELER

When papa Pedro Roldán set up his Sevilla workshop to make religious sculptures, he had no idea how useful his own gene pool was gonna be. The older kids—two brothers and a sister, María—did the heavy lifting, producing rough forms out of terra-cotta and wood. Francisca, another sister, concentrated on painting. But **Luisa Roldán,** nicknamed "La Roldana," was the standout. Her talented fingertips and chisel made her the first female sculptor in Spain. In time, she became a much-commissioned and highly praised artist.

Her specialty was terra-cotta; the item that brought the most *pesetas* in the door, however, was polychromed statue work. Since time immemorial, Spanish churches couldn't get enough of these life-sized images of the Holy Family and the saints. No religious procession in Spain would be caught dead with fewer than ten floats, each with its garishly colored statue, loaded with gilt, alight with candles, dripping with jewels, sallying forth in good-natured rivalry with all the other churches of the parish.

Precocious as an artist, at age fifteen Luisa married another sculptor. In some families, that could have been *la muerte.* However, Luisa had *mucho talento,* and husband Luís, a most un-Spanish male ego.

In 1687, Luisa and Luís headed for Cádiz, where a juicy commission awaited to do some humongous statues of angels and saints for the local cathedral. About this time, the Spanish king, Charles II, heard about Luisa's work, and just couldn't wait to one-up Cádiz. "Come to Madrid pronto—I want you to be my official Sculptor of the Chamber," he said. Luisa immediately cranked out a stunning *Saint Michael and Christ Bearing the Cross* for him.

Even royal sculptors have to eat, however. After famine hit Spain, the king fell into cash-flow difficulties. The royal cafeteria closed, the kingly checks bounced, and it got tough to find a decent tapa at court, much less a meal. When aggressive dunning didn't work, La Roldana and family were reduced to begging.

Finally things got better. Charles died, a new king took over, and Luisa started getting paid. Besides relief sculptures and wooden figures, La Roldana ultimately became best known for her smaller polychrome groups of figures, made of terra-cotta.

In addition to her artistic career, Luisa was a mom—and passed down her magic-fingers DNA to son Tomás. By the time she died in 1704, three generations of Roldáns had left an artistic stamp on Spain—a legacy that can still be seen today in Jerez, Sevilla, and smaller pueblos.

HIGH-FALUTIN' PRESSES & PLAIN-BROWN-WRAPPER PUBLISHERS

In the high-techie new fields of printing and publishing, **Yolande Bonhomme** was one of fifty-four Parisian women who competed between 1500 and 1600. She, however, may have been the shrewdest; in business for three decades, she cranked out more than two hundred titles, many of them hot sellers. Functioning as a printer and a publisher, she even distributed and sold her books beyond French borders into other parts of Europe. When the market for religious books of hours died, Yolande knew what to do. Quickly changing gears, she concentrated on regional titles and scholarly books.

A more lighthearted approach was taken by the **Widow Trepperel,** who operated an early publishing house for trashy novels. Sometimes under her own imprint, other times with her son-in-law, she pumped out 121 titles. *Mais oui*, in French—the language that invented risqué. (But did she originate the plain brown wrapper?) When widowed, her daughter **Macée** also ran a printing and publishing business—at times, in tandem with her own son, Denis. The Trepperel women just couldn't get enough of ink and presses; by 1545, both Macée and her son had died, so Denis' widow, **Jehanne de Marnef,** stepped up and took over the biz.

After 1570, however, the number of female printers and publishers in Paris skidded downward. About that time, a *beaucoup*-francs contract to print liturgical books was won by a consortium of Parisian printers. Oddly enough, that group didn't include a single independent woman or *femme sole* enterprise—can you believe it?

Stop the presses!
Porn is hot again!

29

OBSCENE AND
OVERHEARD

Frances Stelecrag may not have swung a hammer with the rest of the gang; in fact, she was probably overseeing jobs. But she was the blankety-blank equal to any guy with a tool belt when it came to speaking her mind. Frances was a member of the Brotherhood of Carpenters of London, a guild and benefit society that consisted of "good men (sic) carpenters of men and women." But her good standing slid a notch or two in 1556, when she got called on the carpet for "using ondecent words." The warden of the Brotherhood fined her, her nail-driving husband, and a third guy on the job for "yll words." Frances probably didn't mend her ways or curb her tongue, but at least the fines for such naughty misdemeanors went toward guild dinners and assistance to ailing carpenters.

Like male members, women in the carpenters' guild could train apprentices, buy and sell construction materials, and enjoy the guild's privileges and protections. Did women learn the hands-on skills of carpentering? In some cases, yes. Documents show that during the mid-1600s in England, twenty-one girls were bound as carpenters' apprentices. Once their apprenticeships were up, the girls might pursue the trade—or not. One hard-driving widow and guild member named **Rebecca Cooper** apparently had an open-ended apprenticeship policy. After seven years with Cooper, several of the girls applied for their freedom—Enough already!—and received it. About that time, there may have been some "yll words" as well from the widow Cooper.

Good grief—is that guy
working overtime on my dime?

CUNNING CYPRIOT
CUTS A DEAL

regal young woman from royal families in Greece and Venice, **Catarina Cornaro** married James II, self-made "king" of the island of Cyprus. A minor pit stop on the cruise-ship circuit today, at the time Cyprus was strategic to Italian big shots who were trying to keep the serene empire of Venice *serenissima.*

You thought Jackie O lived under a microscope—Catarina was studied more than the disease of the week. After her new husband dropped dead a year after the nuptials, and a very pregnant Catarina became queen of Cyprus, the Venetians sent a top staffer to "look after" the new queen, acting as regent for her and later, baby James III, who in turn dismayed everyone by perishing after one birthday.

Now a seasoned twenty years old, Queen Catarina showed that she had staying power. Despite intrigues, conspiracies, and the tedious bossiness of hometown politicos, she continued as Cyprus Number One for fourteen more years. From time to time, she got a few strokes: a marriage offer from a nobleman of a brand-name Neapolitan family, for instance. As buttinsky as the Venetians were, she almost felt like marrying the guy, just to yank their chains.

When they heard about the offer, the Venetians were really on edge and sent Cathy's brother to negotiate with her. "Look," he said, "we're willing to put an annual salary of eight thousand ducats on the table, and your very own fiefdom in Italy. All you have to do is sign over your late husband's island to the state of Venice. What do you say?"

Catarina pondered. It'd be good for a change to have a house on dry land that was attached to something, namely a continent. "What about fringes?" she asked.

Her brother laid out the tax benefits, adding, "Your generosity will put you on the famous names of Venice list—and you keep the Queen of Cyprus title!" Having cut a better deal than most royal women, past or present, Catarina set up her own court at Asolo, a hilltop jewel of a place thirty miles inland from Venice.

She presided over a sparkling group, including painter Titian and literary catch Pietro Bembo. He wrote about her court in a best-seller called *Of the Asolonis,* published in 1505. It was translated into Spanish and French and ran through twenty-two editions. The word *asolare,* coined by Bembo, came to mean "sweet idleness" (for centuries, the Italian national motto). By now, sweet idleness was OK by Catarina Cornaro, who got really good at it before her passing in 1510.

The Better to
Eat Chocolate With

very great family worth tabloid-bashing has had a curse, and the **Hapsburg girls** and boys were no exception. The only dynasty to rule for twenty generations without ever having had an actual country, the Hapsburgs' power began with a small dukedom in Austria and spread like crabgrass across Europe via marriage.

The original curse was pretty meager—something about a pregnant peasant girl and a randy Hapsburg teen. But the *true* family curse was The Lip (in point of fact, the entire jaw). Populations of good-sized cities could have taken shelter under a Hapsburg chin. Wobbly and red as cherry Jell-O, The Lip made many males of the family look moronic. So you can just imagine how **Princess Anna of Austria** and all the other Hapsburg Annas, Marys, Elizabeths, and Christines felt when they looked in a mirror.

Among other thankless tasks, Anna married King Louis XIII, produced a Louie heir, and ran France as queen regent from 1643 to 1661. Spanish-born Anna brought new ideas to the French court. Naturally they all tittered when she first lifted a cup of some dirty brown substance to those Austria-sized lips. But Anna persisted, jutting out a chin that would stun Jay Leno into silence. The drink she introduced—hot chocolate—eventually became the only beverage fit for the Beautiful People to quaff, once she got the hang of adding sugar to it. For ages, the drink was deemed to be an aphrodisiac in the bargain. Olé! for Queen of Chocolate Anna, who gave women of the world the serotonin-loaded solace they so desperately needed.

Hapsburg bride sets a trend—male masks to cover those pathetically small chins.

A WINNING WAY WITH AN ARIA

hey survived the plague, Italian machismo, and courtly rivalry for their services as intense as any corporate takeover. Who were they? **Francesca and Settimia Caccini,** the most musical sisters to grace the Renaissance. Born respectively in 1587 and 1591 to a talented Florence family, the Caccini siblings ate and drank arias, motets, and canzonettas. (Well, OK, they downed their fair share of rigatoni and pesto, too.)

Dad Giulio, one of the creators of solo singing, the "new music" of the day, pushed the girls hard. Taught singing and composition, Francesca also got proficient on the guitar, harp, and keyboards. At thirteen, she performed with a group her dad modestly called "the women of Giulio Caccini," which included her stepmother and later, her sister Settimia.

After doing a quick tour of France's royals, offers for Francesca as a salaried court singer came pouring in. Queen Marie de'Medici wanted her so badly that she threw in a thousand-scudi dowry as a signing bonus. Amid the clamor of other offers, Francesca bought local, accepting a post as the highest-paid musician at the Florentine court. (Marie, eat your heart out—this offer included a dowry *and* a guaranteed 100 percent hunky court singer husband.)

Now married, and between duties as singer and teacher, Francesca began composing. In 1607, her first commissioned work

The Liberation of Ruggiero: title page of the first opera written by a woman.

37

hit the stage on a high note: a *very* high note. Composed for castrato voices, *La Stiava* was described as "stupendous music." Talk about sleepless in Florence; this gal was a nonstop composer, producing huge collections of music (much of it lost, sadly) and *The Liberation of Ruggiero*, the first opera by a woman, which is still performed today.

Called "proud and restless" by contemporaries, Francesca did her share of envelope-pushing. She produced several works with eyebrow-raising feminist themes, then feuded with a court poet over his callous sexual abuse of female singers ("What are you getting so hot about, Francesca—they're just chicks singing backup!"). Caccini survived the birth of two children, the death of two husbands, and the death of almost everybody else during three plague years. She triumphed as a musician into her fifties, ending her career on another high note by singing duets with her lovely teen daughter **Margherita** for four years.

Also much cooed over, sister Settimia had court singer jobs (with "suitable husband" signing bonus) dangled before her, until settling on the Medici court in 1609. Oops, what's this—Settimia and singing hubby suddenly stalked off the job with no notice. In a demi-quaver, they were snapped up by the celeb-hungry Gonzagas for the court at Mantua. Also a composer, Settimia wrote gracefully melodic music, more like Caccini Lite. She managed to stay on the ducal payroll until she was seventy—a tribute to the deserved fame of the family pipes.

The Tip of The Talent Iceberg

y husband never lets me out of his sight" was a nonstarter in the Dutch household of **Johanna Koorton Blok,** whose marriage to her mysteriously laid-back Mister was low maintenance and long distance. Johanna sang. She painted. She did embroidery and paper cutouts. She etched designs on goblets. What's more, she ran through her repertoire in front of rapt audiences around Europe. Over the waning years of the seventeenth century, Johanna could be found, traveling as a court artiste, giving command performances for royalty in England, Belgium, and Russia. Sometimes she strutted her stuff pro bono; but at least once, Johanna got a cool four thousand florins for a coat of arms she painted for the Empress of Germany. Koorton may have been looked on as a dilettante. Still, the knowledge of her success makes you wonder—how many other women, now forgotten, may have been buzzing around Europe doing the very same things?

hooked on speed

If artists were racehorses, their fame and fortune depending on velocity, Italian painting phenom **Elisabetta Sirani** would have taken the Triple Crown. This full-speed-ahead technique wasn't her idea, however. Blame it on Sirani Senior. Like an arthritic jockey, Giovanni Sirani whipped his daughter on to the finish line. He had her painting dawn to dusk, six days a week. In her seventeenth year, this teen finished five major works, including several commissions for big religious pictures. Dad pocketed the pay, accepted lavish gifts from clients, and stored them away for brag-and-tell.

Where Elisabetta found time to teach students and her two sisters, I don't know. But she did. Her upstairs studio was crowded with women and girls of artistic ambition—with Giovanni taking tolls. Heads of state, royalty on the ramble, and collectors began to fall by casa Sirani, to place commissions and watch her work. Those who still hadn't seen her, had a hard time believing she could paint so fast, so well, and so much (over 180 works in her lifetime).

To quash the rumor mill, on May 13, 1664, the family sponsored a "C'mon You Doubting Thomases" Paint-a-Thon. Drawing from a live model for an international group of curious luminaries, Elisabetta completed a major portrait in one day. To drop-dead applause.

Which was what *she* finally did, on a hot August day in 1665. For months, she'd suffered stomach cramps and been bedridden, then recovered enough to paint again—only to collapse and die in agony.

Predictably, her painter pop screamed, "Poison!" and had the maid hauled off to court. When the servant was found innocent, the Siranis called for an autopsy. According to witnesses, the stressed-out young painter's stomach was riddled with holes—leading art historians to surmise that Elisabetta most probably died from bleeding ulcers: Death by Parental Ambition.

A DOWNRIGHT
BEWITCHING DOWRY

uring the witch-happy Ren centuries, it didn't matter whether you were a filthy rich heiress or a poor granny who happened to look cross-eyed at someone's cattle on a bad day: anyone with XX chromosomes stood a good chance of a sorcery accusation.

No one was safe—not even the queen of England. Take Spanish-born **Joan of Navarre,** a sweet-tempered French royal who put up with nine children and numberless tantrums from the duke of Brittany, her first husband, only to end up nursing "no prize either" Henry IV of England, her second spouse.

Joan's marriage to thirty-six-year-old widower Henry made her queen of England in 1403—and instantly unpopular. You thought the English dumped on Joan of Arc—*this* poor Joan got trashed as a money-grubbing Frenchie. True, she'd brought her own national debt in the form of thousands of French refugees from Brittany. (When she married Henry, she and her followers became as popular as the plague, and were expelled by Brittany politicos.)

Henry, meanwhile, was busy-busy-busy quelling revolts, then became pretty revolting himself, what with a terminal case of eczema and his grand mal epilepsy. Choking back a retch, Queen Joan nursed him for ten years until he died. And what thanks did she get?

Before the king was cold, his son Henry V revved up the Hundred Years' War, which was showing signs of flagging. By 1419, he felt peppy enough to hit his stepmother with a cockamamie charge: She'd brought about itchy twitchy Henry's death through witchcraft, and practiced the black arts against him, her stepson.

Was this curtains for Joan? More like vertical bars—a semi-luxe lockup. Rather than toasting his stepmom on a bonfire, Henry wanted to flambé her bank account. That darned war of his was expensive. As the young ruler was fond of saying, "If we're gonna make it last a hundred years, we're gonna need resources!" By charging the queen with sorcery, he got to sequester (hold *and* use!) the dowry that Queen Joan had brought to England—a tidy 10 percent, give or take a groat, of the entire gross revenues of his government.

So witchcraft it was. Joan remained a prisoner, treated with that teeth-grinding politeness the English use when they really really dislike someone, for three years. In 1422, the king fell unexpectedly ill, repented of his Joan-abuse, and set her free. Luckily he returned her goods before dying. For the next fifteen years, Joan lived in peaceful obscurity at Essex, while the world outside her gates went for a war longevity record. She was the only English queen to be officially charged with witchcraft, and punished for it. Unlike most accused witches, she never got a trial—and afterwards, not even a "Gee, we goofed!" notice.

MINORING
IN SORCERY

Evidently, 1611 was a slow year, penance-wise, in Spain, so Catholic officials decided to proclaim a Year of Grace— 365 days of amnesty when a guilt-ridden witch or two could confess, cop to satanic sex, midnight broomstick rides, anointing with dead baby fat, and heinous acts performed on friends and neighbors, all without suffering a one-way trip to the torture chamber or the Big Burn.

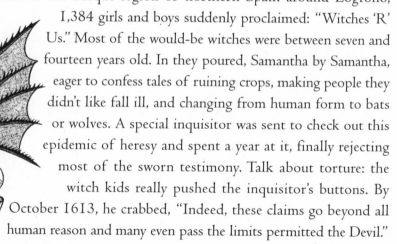

What happened next had church officials stunned, to say the least. In the Basque region of northern Spain around Logroño, 1,384 girls and boys suddenly proclaimed: "Witches 'R' Us." Most of the would-be witches were between seven and fourteen years old. In they poured, Samantha by Samantha, eager to confess tales of ruining crops, making people they didn't like fall ill, and changing from human form to bats or wolves. A special inquisitor was sent to check out this epidemic of heresy and spent a year at it, finally rejecting most of the sworn testimony. Talk about torture: the witch kids really pushed the inquisitor's buttons. By October 1613, he crabbed, "Indeed, these claims go beyond all human reason and many even pass the limits permitted the Devil."

Luckily, the Catholic Church kept a sense of humor—and absolved all 1,384 kids. This lemming-like migration to falsely confess makes a strange contrast to a later phenomenon: between 1611 and 1640, over seven thousand Spanish women would be accused of being witches—and the lion's share of those charges would be brought by young adolescents.

GOITER GLAM—GO FIGURE

An Italian export, and yes, one of *the* Medicis, **Marie de'Medici** queened it over France—not once but twice, first as wife of King Henry IV, and later, as behind-the-throne mom to Louis XIII. She didn't really like the way her husband ran the country—but she didn't have to put up with it long. Henry got assassinated in 1610, Marie stepped up as regent for baby Louie, and spent the following decades reversing her dear departed's policy decisions. Some of the nobility grumbled, but Queen Mom knew just what to do: she drained the coffers to give them fat new pensions. Marie was really lucky. During her sixty-eight years, the strangest thing happened—goiters became fashionable. Since Marie had a beaut, wobbling under her well-fed chin, she became ipso facto a reigning beauty. For her marriage, Peter Paul Rubens even painted her goiter; it, and the rest of her face, repose in the Louvre Museum.

INTERNING AS 007

ooking at this long tall drink of water with the auburn hair, bold manners, and handsome, albeit pockmarked, face, you wouldn't think "good spy material." **Jane Whorwood** was just too conspicuous. Nevertheless, this twenty-seven-year-old wife and mom became an unlikely spy and go-between in the English Civil War between the royalists and the Parliament rebels.

Beginning in 1647, King Charles I was held in very protective custody by the English army at a series of castles. Being that laughable object, a "mere woman," Jane could visit him freely, bringing money, letters in cipher, and suggestions from astrologers as to the best escape route, celestially speaking.

Emboldened by her ability to get to his Royal Captiveness, Jane read up on her Houdini, then brought the king a stash of nitric acid to weaken the window bars, and a file to cut them. Most of the acid spilled before nearing any bars. Still, the visit wasn't a total loss. Whorwood was able to convey yet more messages from astrologers about "the most favorable hours" to schedule talks with the people holding King Charles captive.

By now it was well into 1648. Whorwood tried another escape attempt; during this heartbreaker, she almost helped the king slip away on a ship to Holland. Although no one—Jane included—actually sprang the guy, she kept on trying. What she got for her pains was a growing reputation as the king's mistress—and a nice hug from Charles himself, before he went to his death by execution in January of 1649.

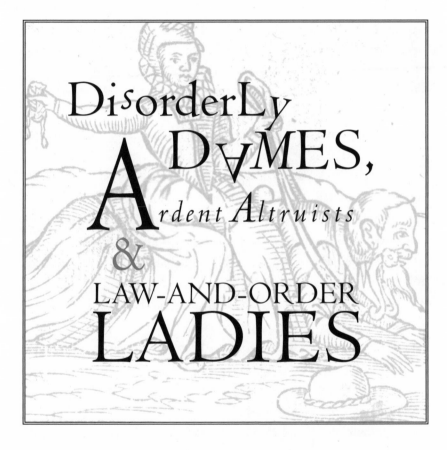

DisorderLy ADᐯMES, ᐯrdent Altruists & LAW-AND-ORDER LADIES

A STAB (OR TWO) AT A NEW LIFE

During those dreary days of February, there's nothing like a juicy murder to take your mind off the weather. In 1550, the English got some truly gossip-worthy mayhem. Southeast of London, in the district of Faversham, a body—riddled with stab wounds from more than one dagger, it appeared—had been found. It was Thomas Arden, a member of the petty aristocracy, and a bit of a rotter.

Soon the story emerged: wife **Alice Arden,** an organized sort of murderess, had enlisted the help of her lover, one John Mosbie, to do the sanguinary sieving. Others might complain about the quality of household help, but Mrs. A. never had that problem. Mosbie was one of the staff. The two lovers also persuaded servants Black Will and Shakbag to assist, and a maidservant to stand by. Once word got out around Faversham about the hit, some local ne'er-do-wells who were friends of the servants actually asked if they could join in on the communal killing! Where Thomas Arden was concerned, to know him was to hate him, apparently.

Once under way, the trial drew a fabulous amount of attention, given the high social profile of the victim, to say nothing of the X-rated amount of sex and violence surrounding the case. Soon it was all over but the sentencing.

The local thugs who'd joined in on the "pin the dagger on the Arden" fun were merely hanged. But the charge against Alice Arden and her servants was more than murder—it was "petty treason against the master"—a far more heinous matter. Thus Mosbie and the two menservants got hanged, drawn, *and* quartered. In this ever-gallant-to-females age, the maidservant and Alice Arden got off with lighter sentences: they both had a date with a bonfire at Canterbury.

In the 1633, a dramatic work called *Arden of Faversham* was published by a female printer named **Elizabeth Allde,** then played to full houses at a London theatre —which goes to show that when it came to crime, homicidal Tudors were tops.

Plunge in, everybody!

GLASS CEILING
IN CELL BLOCK FIVE

Paralleling the late twentieth century, the "Let's lock 'em up" prison industry was booming in mid-1600s Germany. Criminals normally went into lockup one by one. Incarceration employees, however, rarely worked solo—most often, they operated as married couples, giving a spuriously cozy air to corrective institutions. They were even called "father" and "mother" as part of their titles, giving a mom-and-pop air to the place.

Gesche Heimb was the rare exception. A clear standout when it came to being in charge of behind-bars behavior, she got into middle management at the Zuchthaus or house of discipline in Hamburg. As *oeconome* or household manager, Gesche's main mission was to feed the prisoners. With the resident staff, she lived in the prison and directed others' activities. During the day, the prisoners worked on chain gangs, sometimes building the prisons in which they were to be incarcerated.

Despite the dreary surroundings and the lack of eligible (or at least unmanacled) men, romance blossomed for Gesche. Some nine months after she became household manager, she wed a fellow named Jacob Schumacher. Being a Mrs. was fine, but it had a downside: her new spouse, Jacob, jumped up the correctional corporate ladder and became the new *oeconomus.* Was Gesche merely peeved? Or driven to dark deeds? We don't know—but the notice of Jacob's death five months later does seem awfully convenient. Mastering her grief, the freshly widowed Schumacher briskly began acting as sole household manager for nearly two years.

Career-wise, however, Gesche had encountered der dreaded glass ceiling. When the Hamburg Zuchthaus bigwigs eventually learned that Gesche had no intention of playing house in the Big House, they brought out the Golden Handshake. Gesche Heimb Schumacher got a nice pension, a letter that explicitly said, "Incompetence? *Nein!* Und job well done," and the best wishes of the Hamburg prison administrators—who promptly turned around and hired a mom-and-pop to take her place.

EXIT LAUGHING

With high hopes, a German magistrate's daughter named **Kathy Krapp** entered the marriage sweepstakes. Her scatological surname was something of a drawback; still, this was farm country, and Kathy did manage to find a former monk as a fiancé. Phil Melanchthon feared he'd be committing bigamy, since he was "already wedded" to scholarship. Kathy ignored his tremors, gave him a housefull of six children, fed him up like an Iowa porker, and even coaxed her delicate egghead into tasks like cradle-rocking.

An earthy woman who loved nothing more than a good laugh, Kathy kept their house jammed with guests. Only when the decibel level of their hilarity exceeded that of a rock concert did Philip issue a protest. Both Kathy and Phil were generous to a fault. It rarely occurred to them to pay bills; but let a family in need show up at the door, and whatever the Melanchthons had was theirs. At times Kathy had to hock the gifts they'd been given. And so it went for thirty-seven years. When Katherine Krapp Melanchthon died in 1557, a shattered Phil mourned, "I shall not be long in joining her."

FORGET CARDINAL RULES—
SHE RULED CARDINALS

s the folks in seventeenth-century Italy knew full well, you couldn't put your full confidence in a pope named "Innocent." Number eight, for instance, was the first pope to openly acknowledge his illegitimate children. Pope Innocent X, who commanded the big chair between 1644 and 1655, followed in the time-honored sleaziness of his papal predecessors.

Olympia Maidalchini, one of Innocent X's not-so-innocent relatives (and according to some accounts, his mistress as well, thereby efficiently combining two mortal sins in one) privately ran him ragged. Notorious Olympia, also known jocularly as "the papessa" or lady pope, had a nice little sideline business at the pope's digs in Rome. Instead of dashboard figurines or "I survived the Vatican" tee-shirts, she sold *curias,* the offices of the cardinals who resided in Rome and made up the papal court—a body resembling the U.S. Senate. (Same perks, too: optional concubines.)

Maidalchini's abilities at curia peddling were nicely offset by her talents as a poisoner. To open a job vacancy when none happened to be available, Olympia turned to her pharmaceutical supplier, a fellow named Exili. Thanks to her skullduggery, Maidalchini was able to balance supply and demand for the highest monetary return; you might call her Italy's first economist.

MULTIPLE MOVER
& MEGA-SHAKER

Benvenida Abravanel's name meant "welcome" in Spanish, but unwelcome might have been more like it. Born into a Jewish family so tight with Catholic bigwigs that they were exempted from the royal "Get out of Spain" edict of 1492, the not-about-to-be-token Abravanels elected to leave anyway.

That fateful summer, Benvenida and her family headed for Italy, the Abravanels' next home. They had nine carefree years until 1541, at which time Jews were expelled from Naples. Next stop, the nearby jewel of Ferrara, where the Abravanel clan got to stay put and prospered. Already well-educated and married to her first cousin, Benvenida emulated other rich noblewomen and set up her own court. Her circle attracted scholars and artisans, as well as the Bright Young Things in both Christian and Jewish political and business life.

No retirement for Benvenida when she became a widow in 1547—she took over the family import/export business. From her Naples days, she'd become close friends with head honcho Pedro de Toledo and his daughter Leonora. Benvenida became her mentor; the girl came to call her "mother" and turned to her for advice. When Leonora grew up, she married advantageously and became the

Duchess of nearby Tuscany—which was a major break for Benvenida, who knew it's not what you know, but who you know. (That maxim went double for Jews, who were always in the precarious position of being poised for flight.)

When rumors of Jewish expulsion began in the Tuscany area, Benvenida appealed to her young friend—and somehow, the order to expel suffered an amazing delay, even for Italy. In the meantime, Benvenida won key commercial privileges. A good thing too, because the widow Abranavel needed that dough for a religious project. She developed a rave about a brand-new messiah, a genial huckster named David Reuveni. To welcome him to Italy, she made a fabulous banner of gold and silk, and provided other largesse. (David would prove to be just another false messiah, unfortunately.)

Besides her personal piety projects, Benvenida gave to the Jewish community. She personally ransomed more than one thousand people held captive in cities that had turned hostile to Jews. Like her contemporary, Jewish philanthropist and businesswoman **Gracia Mendes,** Benvenida became famous in Israel for the monies she donated. In one of history's small coincidences, Benvenida died in 1560—more than likely the same year that the Jewish world community lost Gracia, that other towering female figure of the Renaissance.

peace queen,
sainthood at eleven

For a woman who only survived to be twenty-six, **Jadwiga of Poland** crammed a lot into her résumé: a tenure as queen, a court battle, and an array of pious activities that won her sainthood. Betrothed at ten to her favorite dancing partner and royal playmate Wilhelm of Austria, she was crowned "king" of Poland the year after. But dirty Polish and Hungarian politics soon threw a monkey wrench into the marital plans. Forget Wilhelm, her nobles pressured. Hook up with Jagiello, the king of neighboring Lithuania—a thirty-five-year-old pagan who loved violence and had a face only a Lithuanian could love. (And those were his *good* points.)

Begging her mom didn't get Jadwiga off the hook. Neither did the fancy gifts that lovesick Wilhelm sent. In desperation, the twelve-year-old tried and failed to break out of her castle. No dice. In 1386, the Lithuanian diamond in the rough arrived, got the Christian name of Ladislaus, and married Jadwiga.

The female half of this odd couple began to be won over when her new groom honored his commitment to bring Christianity to Lithuania by cutting down a priceless stand of ancient oak trees and building a Catholic cathedral on the spot. Soon known as the peace queen, Jadwiga ripped around, making truces with the Hungarians, inspiring the faithful, setting up the Jagiellonian University, and keeping her husband's family from ripping each others' throats out. From time to time an ugly rumor surfaced about her and old sweetheart Wilhelm. Tired of using the "just good friends" line, Jadwiga finally took the rumormongers to court and got her name cleared at a public trial.

The only thing lacking in her life was a child and heir. In 1399, however, a rabbit finally died in Poland and the ecstatic couple started painting the nursery. With tragic swiftness, the premature baby followed the rabbit into the grave, followed a week or two later by Queen Jadwiga. All of Poland mourned the plucky queen—even her lunky husband, who'd been given deathbed instructions ("Here's your to-do list, and you're to marry Anna, the granddaughter of Casimir the Great—now don't forget!") by his awesomely organized wife. You'd better believe that the sainthood cult for Jadwiga (often called Hedvig outside of Poland) began promptly.

Sainthood's tough—you might even have to marry a Lithuanian.

59

ROUEN'S LEPROSY CONNECTION

nfant abuse? Trafficking in body parts? Sounds like twentieth-century America, but it happened in fifteenth-century France, where **Perette of Rouen** had just put in twenty years as a midwife. Out of the blue, another midwife sidled up, asking, "You got any leftover stillborns? I know a noble with leprosy who'll pay big time for one."

After a shocked "Non!" from Perette, the other gal hit on a more obliging colleague. At length Perette reconsidered and agreed to act as go-between. It's still helping people, she rationalized: as anyone knew, rubbing the fat of a stillborn babe on a leper's face was guaranteed to improve the complexion 200 percent. Her first corpse delivered, Perette waited for payment and fantasized about endorsements.

Instead of money, however, she and the bodysnatcher got locked up. Two months later, they spent twenty-four painful hours in the local pillory, then had their midwives' licenses yanked. Perette's plummet into crime had a happy turn-around, though. The hundreds of moms she'd helped deliver over two decades now helped her petition the king. In 1408, she got back her license to practice—which she did, without further abuse or hint of leprosy facials, until her death.

ENCHANTMENT FOR HIRE

From goldsmith's wife to gold digger—no muss, no fuss, no divorce! One of the most successful royal mistresses England has ever known, **Jane Shore** used her beauty and merry wit to give King Edward IV some very enchanted evenings, beginning around 1470—all the while signing in as Mrs. William Shore.

King Eddie spotted her while browsing in the Shore retail outlet. Even after Jane's husband caught them smooching amid the 24-carat, he kept mum. A good time was had by all, until king and husband died—whereupon Jane looked for a lower-profile noble. Just when she'd found a shore thing as a marquis' mistress, new king Richard III butted in, accusing her of sorcery! And just because she'd told old Crumplin' Dick to buzz off, the king made poor Jane do time, followed by barefoot public penance as "a common harlot."

Undismayed and still looking good, Jane turned forty with another triumph: an engagement to Thomas Lynon, the king's own attorney. But the marriage failed to jell, and Jane's fortunes started falling faster than gold futures on the commodities market. Now penniless, she was ready to meet her maker. But she kept on living. Decade after decade. In her eighties, an exasperated Jane finally said, "Enough is enough," lay down in a ditch, and died in 1527—a public figure to the very last.

hot links high jinks

In the spring of 1346, if you found yourself in downtown London and happened to stand downwind in the unrefrigerated vicinity of the butchers' stands, you'd soon know why spices and perfumes were so desperately sought by Renaissance folks. On this particular May day, however, the general stench seemed no worse than usual to **Agnes le Ismongere,** a freelance butcher and purveyor of pork and other meats.

She'd gotten a really good deal on a dead sow from wholesaler John Gylessone. After paying four pence for a selection of raw and cooked chunks, she'd placed the pork on her hot-diggity-dog stands around the city, and watched it fly off the shelves. Then some keen nose happened to make a purchase. In short order, Agnes was getting grief from a queue of squeamish customers with reeking returns in their hands.

It must have been a slow news day. In any event, Agnes and her wholesaler were dragged before the mayor, the sheriff, and what was described as "an immense number of the congregation" in a civil trial and charged with "selling putrid and stinking meat in deceit, and to the perils of the lives of persons buying the same."

The wholesaler admitted that he'd found the sow dead in a ditch in a London suburb. After dressing it out, he'd cooked some of it and sold the decomposing pork to Agnes and other freelancers. A meaty misdemeanor, declared the court, and promptly sentenced John to be slapped in the pillory at Cornhulle. Then the sheriff dug up the skin of the dead sow (you can imagine what state it was in by now), and burnt it at John's feet while he was being pilloried. Talk about cruel and unusual!

Throughout this ordeal, Agnes stoutly stuck to her story that the "said meat of the sow seemed good and proper when she bought it." Despite her obvious shortcomings in the olfactory department, Ms. Ismongere was acquitted—another triumph for the little people.

REBEL NURSE AND
NEWSHOUND

et stuck with mere bandage rolling and bedpan schlepping? Not bloody likely, said London's **Elizabeth Alkin,** who took on a leadership role in the civil war between monarchy supporters and "Kick the royals out!" Parliamentarian rebels that hotted up England around 1647. In her nonstop troop nursing, Liz carted the wounded from the battlefields to an ad hoc facility she set up in London, where she could look after them properly. This Flo Nightingale prototype even found time for pampering, using her spare moments to mend bullet-ridden clothing and give haircuts. ("It's so important for a soldier to feel good about himself, and his appearance.")

Although she often dug into her own monies to minister, Elizabeth Alkin was no Red Cross volunteer. She got regular payments, including a brand new house, from the grateful higher-ups of the Parliament rebel forces. And when she shouted, "Send me more candles and hammocks for the troops!" they listened.

As the war wound down, Elizabeth did too. She wasn't as spry as she'd been on the battlefield, having put on a few pounds. Still game for a game, in her fifties she became a spy for the winning Parliament side that was now running the government. Her assignment? To sniff out any remaining newspapers with subversively royal leanings. To accomplish her mission more effectively, she took on the dirtiest job of all: she became a *journalist*.

In due course this multifaceted mole proudly wore, like a Band-Aid of honor, a nickname she'd been given by both sides in the conflict: "Parliament Joan."

VARMINT VANQUISHER

ome people called this English blueblood "my Lady Anne." To villains, however, she was **"Sheriff Anne Clifford."** In 1605, her pop, the earl of Cumberland, died, and she inherited the office he had held. Like in the Old West, Sheriff Anne had to fight for her office with male heirs, a messy will, and other obstacles. It took more than four decades before she could put on that badge.

By this time, Anne was already good at dealing with varmints—the biggest being her husband, the earl of Dorset. When she'd become rich through an earlier inheritance, her ever-loving tried to get his hands on that lovely lolly, using tactics like depriving her of their daughter and banishing Anne from her own home. None of these subtle methods worked.

After Anne finally moseyed on up to northwest England for her official swearing-in at the beginning of 1650, she hired a deputy and started work. Four times a year, she entertained the area justices of the peace, riding to greet them on a handsome white stallion. Anne Clifford faithfully served as sheriff until the year of her death in 1676: signing writs, reporting on election results, making public proclamations from the king and queen—and keeping those black hats and greedy husbands outta Westmorland.

This law-and-order lady was no token female, either. From the thirteenth through the middle of the nineteenth centuries, England had a number of shires or districts where women handled this hereditary office.

You call that a uniform?
Where's the badge?

"DEAD RIVALS IN ABOUT AN HOUR"

ssassination by toxin, from sweet powders that hid the taste to poisoned letters, was the most popular way to do in your relatives or rivals during the Renaissance. Most of the attention and credit has gone to big names like Lucrezia Borgia and her male family members. But the serial poisoner par excellence was a Frenchwoman named **Catherine Deshayes de Monvoisin,** whom everyone called "La Voisin."

In the last quarter of the seventeenth century, when La Voisin got her start as a street-corner sorceress selling love potions and throwing the occasional Black Mass, she had no idea how good her bad thing would become. When she added nearly undetectable poisons to her stock, she tapped into the huge would-be royal mistresses market. Soon her "Dead rivals in about an hour" campaign began to pay off. La Voisin grew filthy rich.

By the time she had to pay the piper for her toxic activities, La Voisin was practically a franchise. During her trial in 1679, she implicated some 440 people (mostly female) who'd used her nostrums to do in superfluous husbands and romantic competitors, in what was called "a political conspiracy at the highest level." Just hearing about all the near-misses on kings and queens gave the Paris public a delightful *frisson* of fear.

The trial, run by a secret tribunal of judges, lasted three years. At the end of it, thirty-six big names—most of them royal mistresses or former lovers—got death sentences. An additional three dozen got banished or sentenced to hard labor. And the center of this web of intrigue? La Voisin herself had the distinction of being burned to death at a public execution in February 1680.

The trial also made the writing career of Francois Ravaisson, whose eleven-volume work on the evil doings of La Voisin and fellow sorcerers sold like mad to French royalty groupies.

Among the bevy of lethal beauties who used La Voisin's services were the five **Mancini sisters.** These glamorous siblings graced royal courts in France, England, and Spain, mistressing and marrying up where possible. The Mancinis did their collective best to thin out populations at a variety of courts with Voisin's potions; several were banished as a result of the trial. The mercenary mobility and intriguing talent of the Mancinis (but not their penchant for poisoning) would later serve as inspiration for a famous twentieth-century family of sisters—the Gabors.

Truth in advertising—
poison label in La Voisin's day.

69

BAWDY BASKETS & OTHER
STURDY BEGGARS

We want to live without working" was the motto of Renaissance slackers, an army of able-bodied souls who chose to rove and live by their wits—and on the gullibility of others. Women, too, fought for the right to join their ranks.

After the English Civil War in 1646, judges in that land identified twenty-five types of "sturdy beggars," called that to distinguish them from the "deserving poor." (Wars, plagues, and other societal upheavals provided a similar flood of sturdy beggars in other European lands.)

Among the most amusing and infamous were the bawdy baskets—women who ambled from house to house, selling pins and ribbons from the baskets they carried. A bawdy basket was delighted when a child or a servant came to the door—it made her job so much easier. A kid would usually let her in, giving the bawdy basket a chance to case the joint, info which she later sold to a burglar.

Negotiating with a kid was child's play, to coin a phrase. The kid would often end up with a penny's worth of pins, having traded a chunk of bacon or cheese worth ten times that amount. As the name implies, bawdy baskets weren't adverse to selling themselves, either. (They weren't sexual abusers, though; usually they asked for ID to ensure the potential patron was eighteen or older.)

Another female specialty was the "demander for glimmer," who carried bogus papers, "proving" she'd lost her home and possessions in a fire, and preying on good-hearted souls. Your run-of-the-mill demander would take cash or food items for consumption or trade. Since house fires were all too common, there were genuine "demanders for glimmer" on the road, too—and kindly folks gave to both.

Looking for an opportunity to explore your dramatic talents? Hate to comb your hair or wear clean clothes? Women with these yearnings became "counterfeit cranks" (fake epileptics) or "Bess O'Bedlams" (fake former mental patients). They worked the crowds at fairs and hangings. Many went door to door, scaring small change out of residents. It took talent (and a bogus release paper) to be a Bess O'Bedlam. ("Bedlam," the nickname for Bethlehem Hospital of London, the first insane asylum in England, was an infamous holding pen for the mentally ill. Not only did the insane get zero treatment, they were on display—and Bedlam officials charged admission! Whips for visitors to use on inmates cost extra.)

Life was high-risk fun and games for sturdy beggars, male or female. In Queen Elizabeth's day, those found guilty of being vagabonds were, in the words of the law, to be "grievously whipped and then burned through the gristle of the right ear with a hot iron." England had a "Three strikes and you're out" for vagabonds, too: on the third bust, a sturdy beggar was hanged as a felon.

NOBLE ENOUGH
FOR A PEACE PRIZE

uring the often-intolerant Renaissance, when those in power would rather tear your limbs off than let you worship whatever oddball sect you fancied, **Jeanne d'Albret** deserves high praise. This heir to the French throne, king's mom, and sovereign of Navarre in Spain, is thought to be the only sixteenth-century ruler who never killed anyone over religion. (She did hang one lousy commander for failing to keep his soldiers from rape, but that was more like a deterrent.)

A youngster who liked to play with pet birds, Jeanne was forced into a political marriage at fourteen. For such a sweet child, Jeanne kicked up quite a fuss. She had to be carried bodily to the altar and later to the marriage bed, where her new hubby, the duke of Cleves, went through the motions by putting his foot (but no other appendage) on the bed while the king watched. In a few years, the political situation had shifted, giving Jeanne an easy-out annulment.

In her second political marriage, Jeanne and Antoine, the duke of Vendome, hit it off. Now a duchess and queen of Navarre, she played house and exchanged baby-talk love letters with Tony. When Jeanne's first baby died, Antoine consoled her, promising to be "the very kindest and most affectionate husband there ever was in the world." Ultimately, the couple ended up with two living children.

At Christmas 1560, Catholic Jeanne gave everyone a surprise gift: "I'm now a Huguenot (a French Protestant)!" A follower of John Calvin, whose doctrines were called Reformed or Huguenot, Jeanne wanted the whole world to convert. Peacefully.

For the next eleven years, however, the couple suffered through six religious wars between Catholicism and Calvinism and four noble families snarling over the thrones of France. Amid assassination plots, party struggles, and bloodshed, Jeanne and Antoine kept their cool. In 1562, it really appeared as though the Huguenots were going to take it in triple overtime. Then Antoine had a midlife crisis. He went radically Catholic, made Jeanne a prisoner in her own quarters, and ripped their son Henry from her custody.

For her part, Jeanne d'Albret became the Switzerland of queens, maintaining a poised neutrality. The tide turned with war number three (or was it four?). In mid-battle,

*Only the Big Names got immortalized
on popular playing cards.*

Antoine (who never did have a very good bladder) stopped to relieve himself on the city walls, got shot, and died.

By 1571, when everyone was thoroughly sick of war, a marriage between Jeanne's son Henry and Marguerite of Valois was proposed as a Band-Aid to the peace treaty. Jeanne hated the idea, but she was outshouted. This graceful loser threw a great wedding, then died of tuberculosis, just in time to miss the kickoff event for another round of religious wars: the St. Bartholomew's Day Massacre of ten thousand Huguenots.

GIVING BACK TO THE COMMUNITY

ike wars today, belligerence in Europe had a by-product: orphans. Nuremberg's **Beth Kraus** was one. Born in 1559 to peasants, orphaned at ten, she became a maid, married, then ran a successful business with her spouse. Now on the upstanding matrons of the city list, Beth was selected to head up the girls' orphanage. There she taught and doctored the kids, supervised staff, and leaned on townsfolk to take her girls as servants, once they'd turned twelve.

As part of her compensation package, the Krauses got to live at the orphanage—a perk that let the couple buy real estate rentals. Over the years, that hobby added up. When altruistic Beth died at eighty, she willed six houses and 127,000 florins to her favorite charity, a windfall that not only helped orphans for generations but became one for the record books: the biggest endowment ever made by an individual anywhere in Germany.

PATRICIDE: A FAMILY AFFAIR

he pampered daughter of Francesco Cenci, an uppercrust Roman lawbreaker who'd never served a day in prison, and fiscally loaded **Ersilia Santa Croce, Beatrice Cenci** didn't seem like a teen headed for trouble. But then her mom died; Bea was just eighteen. Her father was way too busy to grieve; he'd just been charged with assault and sodomy by his mistress and his valet. Cenci calmly pled guilty, meanwhile laying stacks of "victim compensation" cash on the pope. Amid these distractions, Senore Cenci squeezed in a quickie wedding to **Lucrezia Petroni,** then installed the new bride and Beatrice in a lonely castle outside Rome.

Being imprisoned with her new stepmother was a very bad sign, Bea thought. She was right. In between beatings, her father showed his daughter that he had another kinda lovin' on his mind besides newly nuptial. Her brothers were no help in deflecting dad's attentions. In a desperation move, Bea took up with Olimpio, the castle warden. But Dad's vicious behavior got worse. Pretty soon, Bea was muttering, "Whaddya say, let's pull together as a *family* for once and murder pop!" Her stepmom Lucrezia and two of her brothers, all with plenty of scores to settle, joined the conspiracy.

One September night in 1598, Olimpio and a paid assassin did the deed. They drove a nail into Francesco's head, then threw him out a window, where the corpse landed in a tree. The Cenci family members promptly put on mourning clothes, which fooled no one. Police quickly nabbed the killers. A heartbeat later, Bea and the Cencis found themselves arrested.

Accused of patricide, Bea pled innocent. But those torture sessions on the rack got old really fast, and she and the rest confessed. At the trial, an attorney defended both women with a modern-sounding plea that they were driven to the crime by Francesco's vile behavior. Public opinion polls had the female conspirators acquitted ten to one—but Bea and her financially strapped stepmother didn't have the moxie or the money to win over the pope, who had the last word in cases like this.

One year after the lethal all-in-the-family event, teenaged Bea, her brothers, and her stepmom Lucrezia were beheaded in a Roman square—and the pope ("For *me?* You shouldn't have!") collected the Cenci family property. Writers later made heyday out of this papal payday; and Beatrice became the tragic heroine of plays like Shelley's *The Cenci*.

Rats! I forgot to bribe the pope before doing in Daddy.

77

ACID INGESTION—IT'S MURDER

In her tumultuous lifetime, seventeenth-century bad seed **Frances Howard** was the clear front-runner for the "What on earth were you thinking?" award for her marital choices—to say nothing of her colleagues in crime.

Lady Fran was a familiar face at the English court of King James I of Scotland. Then she spotted a close personal friend of the king, Robbie Carr, whom she decided she really must have. To make sure the magic was mutual, Frances made a love-potion pit stop at Forman the court astrologer's, whose "good living through chemistry" concoctions were all the rage.

At the moment, however, she was still married to another Robert: the earl of Essex. In 1613, Frances blithely began a messy disengagement from the earl—an annulment trial on impotence grounds. The Viagra-less earl lost out, and Robbie stepped in.

It was rumored that King James himself had helped the two new lovebirds get together. Which was passing strange, given the king's own passions. Frances soon found it hard to compete with James' hard-breathing letters to Robbie: "Remember that all your being, except your breathing and soul, is from me. I told you twice or thrice that ye might lead me by the heart and not by the nose. If ever I find that ye think to retain me by one sparkle of fear, all the violence of my love will in that instant be changed into as violent a hatred. God is my judge my love hath been infinite towards you."

As if the tragedy of time-sharing her rosy-cheeked Scot weren't enough, Frances also got dumped on by Robbie's best friend Thomas Overbury. A quick visit to astrologer Forman, whose test-tube wizardry extended to toxins, remedied that wagging tongue. After Overbury got locked in the Tower of London prison for a parking violation, Frances found it easy to get his gruel laced with a lethal additive.

But she wasn't quite devious enough. Just two years into their idyll, Frances and Robbie were rudely interrupted by yet another trial: this one for conspiracy and murder of Thomas Overbury. (King James stayed out of this one—burying his head instead in his racy new "King James version" of the Bible.)

Unlike trial number one, this time the verdict didn't go Frances' way. She, Robbie, and two other conspirators were condemned to death. In fact, the only good thing that happened that week was their pardon; Frances skipped away scot-free. And Scot-free as well. While spared the hangman's noose, Robbie had to languish in lockup until 1622.

TINKERBELL, EAT YOUR HEART OUT

arried to a loser whom she soon lost, **Judith Philips** was torn between several wrenching career choices. O, to be an actress—or a fortune-telling witch, perchance? Or maybe a cowgirl (although said job opening was rare in England of the seventeenth century). This cunning woman from Upper Samborne soon found her métier—a scam that satisfied her entire wishlist, and a few fetishes to boot.

In her native Hampshire County, Judith identified the perfect marks: a farming couple who appeared to have just fallen off the turnip truck. These rustics were in the middle of a lawsuit, but still rolling in bucks. Unbeknownst to them, con woman Philips planted a few items in their yard, then paid a visit.

After a highly artistic double-take, Judith "studied" their faces, asked if they had a holly tree near the house and by any chance, were they being sued? At their surprised "Yes," she gasped out the news that (1) their foreheads looked "lucky," (2) they would win their law case, and (3) their yard just happened to be a clearinghouse for the Queen of the Fairies, and loaded with buried treasure. Once she pointed the way to the "proof," and the farmer unearthed a coin plus an angel figurine, the con was on.

After a modest hem-and-haw, Mrs. Philips was persuaded to help them find the Big Bucks. First siphoning a tidy sum up front for her "operating expenses," she sent the farmer's wife to buy loads of fine white linen, twenty-five candlesticks, the same number of gold angel figurines, and a new saddle. At Judith's direction, the farmer's wife then made a "holy place" for the Queen of the Fairies, decorating a room in the house with linens and other paraphernalia.

Am I going to have to use these spurs on you?

The stage set, Mrs. Philips came to the most enjoyable part of her scam. "You two get down on all fours in the yard," she ordered, then saddled up Mr. Farmer for three jolly circuits to the holly tree and back. For maximum credence, further abasement was necessary. So she told the couple to grovel on their bellies for three hours, saying, "Stir not, I charge you, until I come back again," as she headed for her summit with the Fairy Queen. After a tension-building interval, Judith (now tastefully draped in linens) made a cameo as Tinkerbell, complete with incantations, to the shivering twosome on the ground—then cleaned out the Fairy chamber and vanished.

Too embarrassed to let the neighbors know, the farmer put that saddle to further use—and rode like mad to Winchester town, where he got an understanding relative with clout to organize a "hue and cry" (the Renaissance version of a citizens' posse). Despite the adroitness of her airy fairy caper, Judith Philips got lassoed. Ultimately her victim had the satisfaction of seeing his dominatrix get a few saddle sores of her own, as she was whipped through the streets of London for swindling.

she gave at the office

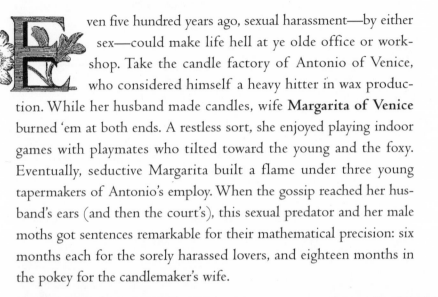

Even five hundred years ago, sexual harassment—by either sex—could make life hell at ye olde office or workshop. Take the candle factory of Antonio of Venice, who considered himself a heavy hitter in wax production. While her husband made candles, wife **Margarita of Venice** burned 'em at both ends. A restless sort, she enjoyed playing indoor games with playmates who tilted toward the young and the foxy. Eventually, seductive Margarita built a flame under three young tapermakers of Antonio's employ. When the gossip reached her husband's ears (and then the court's), this sexual predator and her male moths got sentences remarkable for their mathematical precision: six months each for the sorely harassed lovers, and eighteen months in the pokey for the candlemaker's wife.

Sexual harassment in beautiful downtown Venice.

home girl makes good, does good

oncha love a gal who remembers her roots—and then cares enough to fertilize them? That sums up **Thomasine Bonaventura Barnaby Gall Percival.** Born in southern England's Cornwall, she came from a poor peasant family but ended up as a philanthropist.

How she met her first husband, Thomas Barnaby, is unknown. Suffice to say, she married this well-to-do merchant and not long after, became his widow. Bereft but not completely downcast, Thomasine then hooked up with another short-lived London merchant, Henry Gall. By the time she wed Sir Thomas Percival, who served a term as Lord Mayor of London, Thomasine was rolling in dough. When she lost Sir Tom to the Grim Reaper, she became a very wealthy woman. A woman, it scarcely need be added, with far more black garments in her wardrobe than the average female.

Strangely enough, no children or even stepkids came from her three marital at-bats. Thomasine could have traveled, clipped coupons, or wallowed in her wealth in solitary splendor. But that wasn't her style. She wanted to make life better for others, especially in her home county of Cornwall. When Thomasine wasn't building bridges at Week Ford, she was erecting a free school at Week St.

Mary, or having highways around Cornwall repaired. She also made sure that local maidens got endowed with the right stuff, that is, plenty of cold cash as dowries. Countless Cornish families also got good food and new clothing, thanks to her feeding programs and other efforts.

Widow Percival spent much of her fortune on poor folks and people who got in trouble with the law (often the same individuals, as it happens). Since jails and prisons in Renaissance England didn't furnish many amenities—in some cases, not even basics like gruel and water—she anted up for them.

In her circa-1513 will, she expanded her largesse to help the less fortunate in London, too. Thomasine made sure that the poorest prisoners in every single one of the prisons got food and other basic needs. Her generosity extended to needy Londoners in hospitals and facilities for leper patients. To make sure that poor kids from workhouse backgrounds had a brighter future, she left funds for their education.

Lastly, Thomasine recognized her own good fortune in having found her husbands. In her will, each of them got at least a semi-eternal supply of Masses and prayers said for their souls.

TELL THE HANGMAN THE BUNNY FINALLY LIVED

That old eleventh-hour "death row reprieve" was nothing new to the folks in Northhamptonshire, England. After all, they had **Matilda Hereward** to brag about. A career thief from Branndeston, she and her husband got busted, then convicted of larceny in 1301. Matilda felt nauseated by the whole ordeal; or perhaps that was morning sickness, due to the baby she was expecting.

In June, her hubby took a reluctant two-step to the gallows, where he was hanged. Because of her pregnancy, however, Mrs. Hereward got a "no noose party" postponement. Who knew she was gonna go for a world record? In September, Matilda was all set to waltz up those wooden steps—but the mystified jailer reported that she was pregnant. Again. And returned her to prison.

Thereafter, at six-month intervals, the fecund (or extremely talented simulator) Mrs. Hereward was made ready for hanging, then given the rabbit test. Good grief! Blue again! Matilda managed a total of six stays of execution—and was still alive and kicking two years later.

Clearly, the officials at this particular prison ran a loose ship, since it's doubtful that Matilda, talented as she may have been as a larcenist, could have impregnated herself. Overfriendly jailers? Conjugal visits from friends? Double-bedding with male prisoners? We're left with a tantalizing gap in our knowledge—and a sneaking admiration for a woman who was able to evade, or at least prenatally postpone, her date with the hangman.

REN SPICE GIRLS
HAD HARMONY

arried to a pedigreed yawn named Marco, **Catarucia Zane** wanted more spice in her life as a Venetian Junior Leaguer of the late fourteenth century. Taking a lover was, frankly, trite. But a lover from a lower social class? In this pecking-order-obsessed society, *now* you're talking pungent. To really pour on the capsicum, Catarucia took up with spice merchant Zanino Ursio. (She had a thing for men whose aftershave smelled like basil.)

As a pepper purveyor, Ursio had plenty of money—more than Catarucia's upper-crust spouse, in fact. But socially, Zanino sat far below the salt.

After years of clandestine meetings, the lovers decided to run away. Venice didn't take adultery (or barrier-crossing of social classes) lightly; a reward was offered for their capture, and at length a couple of bounty hunters pinched the pair. Zanino received a year in jail and a token fine; Catarucia, however, got hit with two years behind bars.

After Catarucia had been rotting in jail for a year or so, the city council of Venice agreed to give her an early release, *if* she came up with the scratch to pay her fine—an amount that coincided neatly with the reward that had been offered for her capture.

Being a jailbird, Catarucia was fresh out of lira at the moment. However, **Cristina Dandalo,** her noblewoman friend and neighbor, nobly stepped in. Not only did she pay Catarucia's fine, Cris paid it in her own name—a clear indication that she had cash assets *and* control over how it was spent. Unlike the twentieth-century variety, Renaissance spice girls stuck together. And what could be more liberating than to free a friend—and outrage Venice's elite at the same time.

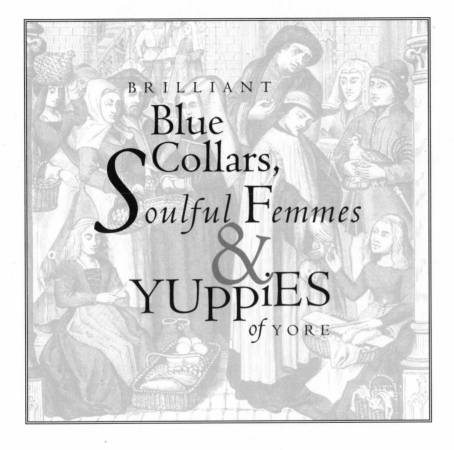

BRILLIANT
Blue
Collars,
Soulful Femmes
&
YUPPiES
of YORE

BOOTSTRAP EDITOR, AUTHOR, & ALCHEMIST

"en and women are equal in everything—except opportunity." That and other acerbic comments came from author **Marie le Jars de Gourney,** who became famous for making her own opportunities. The child of minor aristocrats from a French village, Marie got little encouragement—and no schooling. She ended up educating herself.

This brilliant young sprout then had the audacity to write to Michel de Montaigne, the most important philosopher of her day. Her intelligent fan letter provoked a correspondence that grew into a decades-long intellectual relationship. (You can picture Marie's mom, as the postman arrives with more letters, saying, "When you gonna do something with your life? Get married, for instance?")

Wedding bells weren't part of Marie's game plan, however. In 1593, church bells tolled for Montaigne, and his widow asked Marie: "Would you prepare and edit my husband's work?"

Would she ever! Marie jumped into the daunting task. The job she did editing Montaigne's masses of manuscripts soon made her well known in intellectual circles. In 1597, now the darling of the Montaigne groupies, she did a lecture tour to European cities and was wined and dined as a distinguished visitor.

Heartened by her experiences, Marie headed for Paris to become a woman of letters in her own land—but soon ran out of *le monnaie*. The resourceful Mademoiselle le Jars then turned to something more sure-fire: alchemy. Granted, nobody ever succeeded in making gold (alchemy's main goal) but a good living could be had writing about it, teaching others, and so forth (uncannily like the writing field today!).

It's so hard to get decent help for an alchemy start-up.

Marie had to tread lightly; alchemy bordered on witchcraft. In 1610, over four hundred French women had been burned as witches in Bordeaux province alone. Besides its political incorrectness, alchemy was devilish expensive. Luckily, Marie had a friend with a lab and a furnace. For nearly a decade, she did alchemical research—and possibly got into cosmetics manufacture as a way to supplement her income.

Still socially incorrect by French standards, the unmarried le Jars then wrote two books on feminism in 1622 and 1626. Shocking as it was to her dear old mother, *Equality of Men and Women* and *The Grief of Women* were hits and went into reprints. (Now Marie had a royalty stream, however minuscule.) She began to get writing assignments for articles on feminism, language, poetry, and politics.

Living to a ripe age eighty, Marie became a self-made success in life, and a role model for younger women—from Holland's Anna Maria von Schurmann to England's Margaret Cavendish.

milking multiple markets

alcium-rich **Katharine Elliot** already had a nice gig going as "wett nurse to the Duke of Yorke" (in point of fact, it was the duke's offspring that got the mammary attention). But working for a celebrity client gave her bigger ideas. Emboldened by success, Elliott decided to petition the king of England for a piece of land lying idle that appeared to be royal real estate. "What could it hurt?" she reasoned.

With the help of a rent-a-scribe, she applied for a sixty-year grant on the property, called West Sedge Moor. "Right now it's got squatters on it, but I'll pay rent, at a shilling an acre," she added. Since the royals had yet to get a stinking cent out of West Sedge, this sounded like found money. Mrs. Elliot got a speedy "Yes" to her petition. She was on a roll now; reasoning that her milk supply wasn't going to last forever, she next applied for a grant to sell silk stockings and waistcoats. The savvy La Leche provider even laid out a thirty-one-year business plan, showing her monarch just how much was going to be realized from the sale of each item over the next thirty-one years.

She Turned London
Upside Down

To stand out in a crowd, even a drunken bunch of randy Londoners, you had to specialize. That's what **Priss Fotheringham** did, with her sexual specialty called "chucking." This cat-eyed gypsy girl began her career as a whore with a minor in thievery during the 1600s. Early in life, Priss had a series of bad breaks: smallpox left her face looking like a raisin pudding; then her husband "befrenched her and pockified her bones soundly" (London slang for giving her VD and beating her). After running away with a workman and her husband's cash, Priscilla lost her lover once the drinking money ran out. Worse, her abusive husband charged her with theft, and Priss went to Newgate Prison.

Incarceration turned out to be Priss' first real break. In jail, she met the two biggest pros in the sex business, **Damaris Page** (a.k.a. "the Great Bawd of the Seamen") and "Madam to the stars" **Elizabeth Cresswell,** owner of a discreet and highly successful bordello for English politicos.

"Find a niche!" they urged her. And did she ever. Once freed, Priss opened the Six Windmills brothel, where, twice daily (in the words of a bug-eyed witness), "Priss stood upon her Head with naked Breech and Belley while four Cully-Rumpers chuck'd in sixteen half-crowns into her *Commoditie.*" Commodious must have been the *mot juste* for Priss' equipment—that's a lot of coinage! (For an additional fee, clients could also pour wine into the *Commoditie.* But only the top vintages—they smarted less, noted Fotheringham.)

Alert to further promotional possibilities, Priss soon spotted another merger waiting to be made. She linked her "Chuck Office" with a hot-button site called the "Prick Office," offering the exotic service of fellatio to your normally meat-and-potatoes English clientele.

Business fell off terribly in 1665, when London got hit by the Great Plague. Priss' Six Windmills happened to have an unfortunate site next to a great dunghill—which plague-fleers thought of as an epicenter. Fotheringham survived the plague, the Great Fire of 1666, and later, even a riot on her doorstep between apprentices and nobs. This time, however, they were fighting over another "commodity" entirely—workers' rights. Now that was a cause Priss Fotheringham could get behind.

A RARE OLD BIRD

When his daughter **Cassandra Fedele** showed signs of being smart as a whip, her dad Angelo, an ordinary guy from Venice, had an extraordinary thought: Why not throw the education at her, instead of her brothers? Tutored in Latin, Greek, history, and other high-density studies, Cassandra conquered them all. By twelve, the little humanist began recitations to audiences in Venice and the university nearby. Everybody ate it up.

By now the city mascot, she got invited by the Queen of Spain to join her court. Cassandra said, "Si!" The Venetians, jealous at the thought of sharing, said, "No!" and declared her "too great an asset" to leave. Despite having her passport pulled, Fedele felt good about her fame. By 1491, she had heavyweights like poet Angelo Poliziano putting her on the "top ten ornaments of Italy" list. Mama mia! What could stop Fedele's climb to the summit? One word: birthdays. Once she hit thirty, Angelo's daughter went overnight from a prodigy to an unmarried embarrassment. Under protest, Cassandra was wed to a physician. Then total silence for sixteen years.

In the 1520s, now a widow, Cassandra made news again. But not in the way you'd hope. So much for doctors as providers—her mate died poor, and her own family refused to pony up for their once-illustrious daughter's old age. Fedele began writing to the pope, asking for a "former ornament of Italy" pension. No luck. Somehow she survived to age eighty-two, still writing to popes. Finally one answered. Good old Paul III couldn't cough up cash; he did, however, find Cassandra a job—as head of a church orphanage. A little Italian irony there?

When Cassandra reached ninety-one, suddenly she became a prodigy again. This time it was, "Would you look at the brains on that old lady!" In between mopping up after orphans, she was hired to welcome the queen of Poland with a nice Latin oration. The off-again, on-again famous Fedele would live two more years before disappearing for good, a rare old bird indeed.

BUTTER WOULDN'T MELT
IN HER MOUTH

awking butter and cheese at the retail level was no slice of Stilton, thought **Edith Doddington** of Hillbishops, England. Should she go for the Darigold? Instead of remaining a Regrater (a woman who sold perishable food items door to door), in 1630 Edith applied for a license to be a Badger (more like a food wholesaler). That settled, this energetic widow hitched up her team of horses (the law was strict—she was only allowed three), and set out to bring the best butter and cheese into the counties of Devon, Dorset, Wilts, and Hampshire. Her papers gave Edith license to wholesale her products, then buy (or trade for) corn or grain in those counties and sell it in her own. Being a wholesaler was no holiday. Edith was only street-legal for a year—after which, she had to apply and pay again to be a bloomin' butter Badger.

YOU'RE IN GOOD HANDS

Women don't seem to have played many innings in the insurance game. (Allergic to actuarial tables, perhaps?) But England boasted at least one notable exception—a go-getter preacher's daughter named **Dorothy Petty.** Unlike her lower-key peers, she wanted the world to know about her successes. She set up a London insurance office "in order to serve the Publick, and get an honest Livelyhood for herself. . . . " It may not sound as slick as a State Farm ad, but her words ring with sincerity: "The said Dorothy had such success in her undertaking, that more claims were paid, and more stamps us'd for policies and certificates in her office than in all other the like offices in London besides; which good fortune was chiefly owing to the fairness and justice of her proceedings in the said business: for all the money paid into the office was entered in one book, and all the money paid out upon claims was set down in another book, and all people had liberty to peruse both, so that there could not possibly be the least fraud in the management thereof." Call me crazy, but why don't more business folk today operate like Dorothy Petty?

GLASSY-EYED IN VENICE

Developing local talent and keeping a lid on inflation: that was the political pledge of **Franchesina Sorenzo** in 1341, when she became dogaressa or top dog of Venice alongside her husband Giovanni, the new doge.

Heaven knew, being CEOs of the Most Serene Republic of Venice didn't pay squat. Always on call for endless bridge-opening and canal-blessing ceremonies, she and Giovanni couldn't even accept any thank-you gifts except herbs and flowers.

Her city on stilts was already famous for its local silk industry. In fact, that was one of the few perks of Dogaressa Franchesina's job— the gorgeous silk courtier duds she got to wear around the Palazzo Ducale and to the festivals.

Still, she relished the challenge of building up the local Murano glassmaking industry. After lots of work on Franchesina's part, the glass of Venice became a sought-after prestige item worldwide— all without raising the cost of living at home.

There was a tiny bit of bad news, however: because of the allure of Murano glass, trade with countries to the East quadrupled—bringing lots of ships, ship rats, and a new round of plagues, which by 1348 would wipe out more than half the happy citizens of Venice.

NANNY BY DAY,
ESCRITORA BY NIGHT

Even humble English servants could be voracious readers—and in **Madge Tyler**'s case, writers and translators. Around 1578, she had the audacity to publish a work called *The Mirror of Princely Deeds*, which she had translated from the Spanish of writer Diego Ortuñez de Calahorra. She dedicated it to Thomas, Lord Howard (yes, the same social-climbing family whose marital "successes" included ill-fated queens Anne Boleyn and Catherine Howard) and his parents, who'd been good to her "when she had been their servant." Given her literacy and intelligence, Madge probably worked as a governess for the family. In the book's foreword, Madge first gave the standard mock meek "How dare I" line for attacking "masculine" subject matter. Then she said what was really on her mind: how she delighted in the Spanish language—and planned to translate whatever the heck a woman might want to read.

shrewd shrewsbury

oted for her nearly unbroken string of upwardly tax-bracketed marriages, **Bess Talbot of Hardwick** would have made a smashing Monopoly player. Not only did she get Park Place and Baltic Avenue, this ace land grabber and money lender went home with all the hotels. An English rose of great charm and ability in the art of long and lucrative engagements, Hardwick had 20/15 eyesight when it came down to the fine print of a marital agreement.

Her first marriage, however, was more a case of great timing. When Bess, the no-prospects daughter of a smalltime country squire, was asked to nurse a sick neighbor, she acquiesced. The young invalid turned out to be not 'alf bad once he could take nourishment. She married him—only to have him keel over, leaving Bess his worldly goods. That seed money got her in business.

First, she bought out her brother, who owned Hardwick, their family home. That made her a landowner and one of the gentry—so she could take dead aim at another marital coup. This time, she wed Sir William Cavendish, had lots of boys, and got him to buy more estates before he kicked off. Husband number three came off with military precision. A career soldier, he followed orders well: at his death, all his holdings went to his multi-surnamed widow.

By now she could have kicked back, hung out with the other wealthy widows. But no. Bess wanted to make it to the top. And she did, marrying the most paparazzi-worthy noble in the nation, a veritable Bill Gates of English peers, the earl of Shrewsbury.

Now the Countess of Shrewsbury, she and he had a pack of children: his, hers, and theirs. In time, Bess pulled off a Grand Slam Double-Marriage Family Encounter, linking various Talbots to Cavendishes. Then the countess and the earl began to fight. Since they were mainstays of the English economy, Queen Elizabeth herself stepped in. The patch-ups didn't take, however. Ultimately, Bess stalked off, the family members who'd taken her side trailing after.

The two parties were so filthy rich by now that the divorced countess was left with what amounted to a small country. The founder of the dukedoms of Devonshire, Newcastle, and Portland, Bess had amazing baronial houses and estates everywhere—which, with the help of her second son William, she ably ran. In 1597, she gave Hardwick Hall, her ancestral home, a facelift; the glittering final result contained more glass than any building in England that wasn't a church.

She never read a book, but she knew money: clever Bess paid less in taxes than she gave out each year as gifts! This self-made millionaire was no Scrooge, either. To her dying day, she enjoyed philanthropy almost as much as evading taxes.

Brilliant Blue Collars, Soulful Femmes & Yuppies of Yore

SHE WORE LOTS OF HATS—
AND MADE A FEW

Many a virtuoso of varied talents was described as "a Renaissance man," but few women won that label. **Margaret Baynham** was not a blueblood or a tabloid-worthy tart. But she *was* a Renaissance woman, and did an astonishing number of things. Widowed twice, this Englishwoman conducted business and had property on both sides of the English Channel. In the port city of Calais, France, she ran a charming gabled boardinghouse on the market square, targeted at the business traveler. Instead of in-room faxes, she had a heated counting-house nearby for guest use.

In addition, Margaret farmed hundreds of acres around Calais, and was an import-export trader (often called a stapler) in her free time. Mrs. Baynham dealt in staples like wine, herring, and wool; she raised sheep on both her English and French holdings. A thrifty housewife, she wasn't too proud to spin her own wool and make her own tablecloths and articles of clothing. As a stapler, Margaret also had the legal right to export thirty sarplers or canvas sacks of wool each year out of England. That's 192,000 pounds—a world of wool no matter who's counting it.

Besides her business acumen, Margaret Baynham was a sturdy survivor who'd lost her husbands and numerous other relatives in the plague and other epidemics. Some of Mrs. B's letters have survived, contained within the written accounts of the Johnson family who did business with her. Her words project a homely warmth and sweetness that is still vivid today.

Care to arm-wrestle
for the lunch check?

A PFENNIG MADE
IS A PFENNIG EARNED

urope during **Karyssa Under Helmslegern**'s time was short a lot of things: chocolate, a decent plague remedy, even coins. Due to a severe lack of gold and silver, copper coinage (and alloys like the copper-tin mix called bronze) had extra-heavy use. Karyssa, a native of Cologne, Germany, was the trader to contend with in the mid-1400s. She imported 624 hundredweight of copper at a go into Cologne. Under Helmslegern was no underdog. She cornered an amazing market share: nearly 2 percent of all the copper flowing into this key trade city of Renaissance times. An international trader of heavier metals, Karyssa also handled commodities like sheet iron. At one time, her shipments represented a crushing 5.8 percent of the total exports of the city.

WOAD IS ME

Besides the religious strife of Renaissance times, people like **Katherina Amlingyn** had to endure the wrenching economic rivalry (similar to the Apple–IBM struggle in its intensity) of indigo versus woad. Before indigo came along, the blue dye of choice was woad, a plant with small yellow flowers. Although indigo would eventually become the Big Blue of its day, Europe's still-powerful woad lobby got laws passed in 1581, forbidding the sale of even a smidgen of indigo.

Woad was still queen in the northeast German town of Erfurt during Amlingyn's lifetime, and she was its main maven. She and her daughter, along with several other partners, headed up a trading company that sold the dye-stuff all over southern and eastern Europe. For eight years, they did business without problems.

Then woad woe hit, in the form of a lawsuit from the city of Magdeburg. Their target? Twenty wagonloads of Amlingyn's primo grade stuff that got stopped at Gorlitz, near the Polish border. Did the impetus to sue come from an indigo freelancer? Or some wild-eyed partisan of a woad-free Europe? And where did that huge and costly heap of confiscated woad end up? We don't know the answers to these tormenting questions. However, thanks to the documentation left by the rapacious city council of Magdeburg, we glimpse two generations of businesswomen, struggling with the problems of a fascinating business.

MAMA LOOK AT BUBO

lthough London realtors had a hard time explaining away the creepy abundance of houses for sale after an epidemic, **Meg Blague** found plague to be profitable. During London's worst, the Big Giant Plague of 1665–1667, she worked as Head Matron for the city's famous institution for the poor—the three-hundred-bed St. Bartholomew's Hospital. When the plague really got rolling, it killed thousands per week, out of a total populace of some 250,000. Unlike the timorous physicians on staff, who left the city during the worst of the bubo-bursting, Matron Blague stayed on the job. Her constant care (besides making sure each patient got three pints of beer a day, she supervised the weaving of sheets from flax) earned Meg a commendation and a reward from the hospital governors, who praised "her attendance and constant great pains about the poor in making them broths and other comfortable things for their accommodation in this late Contagious Tymes, wherein she hath adventured herself to the great peril of her life."

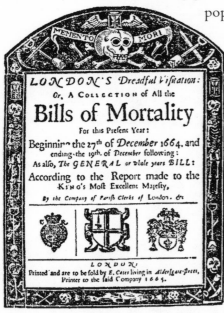

Think El Niño's bad? Try a plague year or two.

CLEANING UP IN CATALONIA

Among Barcelona's 35,000 enthusiastic residents in 1440 was a widow named **Eulalia Sagarra** and her grown son, Bartholomeu, who got along well enough to become capitalist pigs together. Canny in business, the Catalans believed that blood (and the bottom line) were always thicker than water. Mom and son decided to become active partners in a soap company, Eulalia chipping in thirty florins to Bartholomeu's two hundred. Then they bought the raw materials, set up the books, and developed a marketing plan. But something was missing. Oh yes, a soapmaker. After they hired Andreu Dea Brull, the company was afloat. Before long, their first batch of beauty bars was ready for export. At that point, Mother Eulalia might have been called on to apply a little spiritual soft soap of her own—some extra innings at the cathedral, praying to her namesake Saint Eulalia, who happened to be Barcelona's patron and *the* saint to see when it came to protecting ships against storms at sea.

make Lace, not ore

In the 1470s, the cry of "Silver!" rang out in the hills of southern Saxony and northern Bohemia. Soon the rush was on. Mining towns like Annaberg and Marienberg sprang up; men and women poured into the area, wanting work. Gals with good backs even took up mining: they washed and broke up ore; worked in the smelting huts; and carried implements, ore, and coal for the furnaces from one spot to another. Naturally they got paid less than men did. In Freiberg, however, they got to be members of the miners' fraternity—although they were called by the unbecoming name of "old sisters."

When **Barbara Uttmann** was born in 1514, things were still in mid-boom. By the time she became the capable wife of Christoph, a hotshot with lots of mining interests in Annaberg, the silver was petering out. Christoph started coming home with that gloomy "We're losing money" face. Anticipating the day when the Uttmann mines would be nothing more than dead holes in the ground, pragmatic Mrs. U. researched alternative employment ideas. Hmm—how about a job corps for Annaberg's women? With herself as entrepreneur?

Barbara, who'd learned to make pillow lace from a woman fleeing the Inquisition, organized local classes; soon hundreds of housewives had lace-ready status. The women she taught were highly motivated—

and for more than economic reasons. By now, there were countless out-of-work miner husbands underfoot, whining about the "good old days" of being mercilessly exploited. If Barbara hadn't stepped in, there could have been untold domestic homicides in Annaberg.

By the 1560s, the bobbin babes of the lace corps numbered over nine hundred women. Perched on special hard cushions, lacemakers sat at home, whipping out frothy concoctions—and making Barbara Uttmann a rich woman. Lace pillows and other confections being every homemakers' must-have, the finished products found a ready market. Ultimately, Barbara went international. There was plenty of business to go around, too—and Mrs. Uttmann made sure that other entrepreneurs (all of them women) in the Annaberg area got in on it.

At length, the left-in-the-lurch male miners got a clue, too, and began to manufacture trims and braiding. Before you could say "doily," they'd formed a guild. One of their first rules: Braids and trim were male territory—no stinking lacemakers allowed!

Even after she died in 1575, Barbara was remembered for revitalizing her area. And in Annaberg, you can still admire a large statue of her, complete with lace pillow, honoring her vision.

I'm still doing the wash—but at least it's a paid gig.

subpoenaed to death

When she married James Berkeley in 1424 and signed on to become a Lady of the Manor, young **Isabel Berkeley** had no idea she'd have to double as an attorney. But that problem arose later. First she had to cope with running her manor: supervising the staff, directing farm operations, overseeing the making of beer, bread, and clothing, running her own school at times, and doctoring the family and manor workers. That stuff, however, was child's play, compared to the snarl that the Berkeleys got into.

From her wedding day, Isabel looked forward to moving into a new home. Her husband had great expectations from his uncle: the family estate, called Berkeley Castle. By the time he inherited it, the place was bound to need maintenance, maybe a new dungeon, and so forth. But Isabel felt ready to take on anything.

What she didn't count on was eviction. When dear old uncle finally went to his maker, she and James found out that Lord Berkeley had named his only daughter Elizabeth as his heir. Worse yet, in the hustle and bustle of the funeral, Elizabeth and her new husband, the earl of Warwick, had quietly set up a squat in Berkeley Castle and changed the locks.

When James went over to say, "Excuse me, but you lot gotta squat somewhere else," he was threatened with great bodily harm. The earl's ugly behavior soon had Isabel's grown sons and her husband James quivering in a corner.

Time for some decisive action. With a sigh, Isabel put on her city clothes, went off to London and became the family solicitor—acting as attorney for a legal snarl that got more complex by the day.

James and the boys weren't much help; Isabel wrote to them constantly with instructions: "Everything's going fine with the case but for the love of God, send money—else I'll have to pledge my horse and return home on foot. Don't make any deals without me!" To keep the case going, the cash-poor Berkeleys had to put up their furniture as collateral, starting with the uglier items from their private chapel.

You know how it is with family feuds—the case spread faster than Lyme disease at a tick convention. Eventually Isabel had to go all the way to Gloucester to represent their legal interests. Instead of getting Berkeley Castle back, she got a free stay in the dungeon of *another* castle—another dirty trick from the party of the first part.

Isabel's tremendous energies (to say nothing of her pro bono work) were to no avail. She died—or was murdered—in that castle cell, the victim of a legal battle gone very sour. By now, the rest of the Berkeleys had made the case their life's work. Isabel's son William brought a wrongful death lawsuit on his mom's behalf—a pretty, if posthumous, gesture.

LEPER LADIES & OTHER
GALLANT GERM FIGHTERS

uring Europe's major epidemic centuries (1348–1665), there was no quarrel at all about the worst job in the world: plague searcher. (And no surprise as to which sex filled it, either.) One of a corps of corpse gumshoes, the **Widowe Lovejoye** got four shillings per week for her reeking, heartbreaking job. In 1639, she was sworn in by the council of Reading, England, to examine "all the bodyes that shall dye within this borough, and truly to report and certifye to her knowledge of what disease they dyed, etc." As an incentive, Lovejoye and other plague searchers got bonus payments for corpses carried to burial. (Given the gruesome state of the bodies and the fact that most plague searchers were senior citizens, I wonder just how often Lovejoye collected that bonus.)

Speaking of collecting: although the widow did her job impeccably (surviving in the bargain), the council hedged on her salary, offering her a combo of cash, cloth for two garments, and clout—by promising to grease the way for her two foreign-born sons-in-law to be allowed to exit England. Lovejoye squawked at the shortchange. Not until 1641, however, did the council acknowledge her petition, saying, "It was agreed that she shall have thirty shillings as soon as the tax for the visited people (i.e. plague victims) is made up." At those glad tidings, a resigned Lovejoye no doubt sat back to wait for a wintry day in hell.

In those epidemic-rich times, leprosy was another disease on the rampage, sparking a building boom of leper hospitals. Leprosy peaked in Europe around 1300, then slowly declined, overtaken by an exciting new epidemic called tuberculosis (a closely related ailment, believe it or not). While leprosy was still pruning noses and digits, leper ladies like Belgian Beguine **Mary d'Oignies** tended the sick. D'Oignies, who'd given away her wealth to care for the less fortunate, cooked for leprosy sufferers. As a caregiver, she also made sure that each leper had a working bell—the "bad humor man" signal that an infected person was in your neighborhood.

When tuberculosis grabbed the malady limelight in the 1350s, it became a prestige disease, a "romantic" death sentence, especially for upper-class young women. Three of the most popular and written-about females of fifteenth-century Italy were the gorgeously wan and totally tubercular **Simonetta Cattanei Vespucci** and sisters **Albiera** and **Giovanna Albizzi**—all of whom expired before the age of twenty-one.

The High (and Dry) Life

a bella **Julia Lombardo** was a typical midlist courtesan, but even a middle-of-the-strada strumpet in Renaissance Venice had a lifestyle we'd label as sumptuous. In the 1530s, she lived in a house which she'd furnished with sculptures, porcelain, paintings, brass fire-dogs, beautifully carved chests, and those all-important business write-offs—canopied beds and mirrors.

Given the abundance of canals and the lack of terra firma in Venice, your average streetwalker didn't have many streets on which to walk. But female ingenuity prevailed. Julia and the pricier sexual saleswomen adopted a uniquely Venetian venue: a rendezvous for two in a gondola. Of the ten thousand glossy bright gondolas used to get around sixteenth-century Venice, nearly half were rentals. At first the flat-bottomed love boats were open-air affairs. Then some clever soul (probably a damp courtesan fed up with winter drizzle) dreamed up the *felze*, an intimate cabin on board, nicknamed "the shelter of sweet sins."

Besides the floating whorehouse strategy, Lombardo and the thousands of other Venetian vixens for pay had a fashionable new way to keep their feet dry while drumming up trade: the chopine or platform shoe. Shades of the sixties: this footwear, imported from

Turkish harem gals, combined shoes with high-rise painted clogs. The Venetian platform shoes soon wobbled to heights of as much as twenty inches—requiring hookers who wore them to lean on the arms of a pair of servants to keep from making a three-point landing on the slippery cobblestones of the Piazza San Marco.

Yo! Gondolier! Another go-around! And no splashing this time!

her how-to came back to bite her

seventeenth-century Dr. Spock to English moms, midwife and author **Jane Sharp** had thirty years of birthing babies under her apron when she wrote *The Compleat Midwife's Companion.* The first practical manual on the subject in English, her bestseller stayed in print until nearly 1800. Jane didn't mind lifting great birthing tips from the past either—like the teachings of Trotula, famed eleventh-century Italian author.

Jane's goal had always been to upgrade midwifery. Teaming up with **Hester Shaw, Elizabeth Cellier,** and other formidable female forceps wielders, in 1634 the woman had petitioned London's College of Physicians. "Allow us to have a guild, and to teach," they said. "That way, we can educate midwives and raise standards." In both England and France, they got an emphatic "No!"

Blocked by law and male vetoes, Jane turned to writing as a way to improve professionalism—and the mortality rate for newborns, at that time abysmally high. Once Sharp got into print, she got a surprise: male readers. With Jane's manual in hand, any Tom, Dick, or Harry could (and did) pick up a kettle of boiling water and become a midwife. (Were they called "midhusbands," I wonder?)

PASTA CURTAIN
FOR A LEGAL STAND-IN

ovella Andrea's dad Giovanni, a law professor at Bologna, got a kick out of teaching his daughter the ins and outs of torts and trials—so much that whenever he got called away to chase an ambulance, he'd ask Novella to sit in and give his law lecture. Enlightened, this proud papa might have been; still, the 10,000 students at Bologna U. (whose alums included Dante and Petrarch) were mostly male students, and this *was* Italy. Besides her bulging brain, Novella had other, more physical assets. To keep her beauty from blinding (and/or arousing) the audience, she and Dad worked out a strange scenario that had her lecturing behind a curtain. (The titillation probably kept male students awake—but what a disincentive for the handful of female students!) Fond Giovanni also named a collection of lectures after his daughter, whose abilities at teaching law showed how capable women were. A century later, Novella gained literary immortality: she became a role model in feminist **Christine de Pizan**'s *Book of the City of Ladies.*

RENAISSANCE
SLICE-AND-DICERS

Whether they opted to practice surgery, set bones, do herbal remedies, or administer useless and nasty nostrums, female doctors during Ren times were strictly footnote material (and still are, for that matter).

Funny, since the age had such standouts as **Clarice di Durisio,** a licensed Italian surgeon in the early 1400s whose specialty was "women's eye problems." (Exciting to think that female eyes rated their own ophthalmologist, isn't it?)

Or how about **Isabelle Warwicke,** an English surgeon who in 1572 was awarded a license to practice in York with the hearty if ungrammatical words, "She hath skill in the science of surgery and hath done good therein."

Paris surgeon **Perreta Betonne,** on the other hand, had professional woes. Found to have poor Latin skills and gaps in her herbal lore, Perreta had to stand by while the court ripped down her "surgery-while-you-writhe-in-agony" sign. Although witnesses attested to her skill, she was imprisoned briefly. At least Betonne's health care was within the economic reach of anyone; in the slang of the day, she "worked for God," that is, for free.

So how did surgeons put groceries on the table? In England,

France, and Germany, they often were barber-surgeons, who learned to cut off limbs while getting skills at cutting hair, applying leeches, and letting blood. (In all too many cases, the haircuts may have done more good than the surgery.) Instead of country club memberships, doctors got perks like tax-free citizenship in a given city.

Just like today, litigation was a medical fact of life, especially for female doctors; that's how we know about **Elizabeth Heyssin,** a German barber-surgeon. In 1596, Elizabeth started a court battle with her fellow barber-surgeons of Memmingen. She began her career as a "no visible means of support" sawbones, dispensing freebie health care (but accepting the odd chicken, candles, or bedding that came her way). By 1602, though, Heyssin made house calls, had her daughter in medical training, and was allegedly knocking down the salary of a university-trained physician. Even more heinous, she occasionally engaged in urine-sniffing and prescription-writing—medical acts that had local doctors and apothecaries apoplectic.

With some caveats, Dr. Heyssin won her case, and the right to continue practicing medicine. As she argued, "Such activities are done by honorable women, not only here but in other cities as large and important as Memmingen. Such are fitting things for women to do."

RABBIT IN A LONDON STEWE

Some women might dream of brewing or butchery. But the indoor activity that **Joan Hunt** most hankered after was owning a brothel. Not just any cathouse or stewe would do—Joan longed to be a bawd in London's exclusively scuzzy Bankside district. In 1365, she found one for sale that included the sweetener of an indentured servant named Thomas Bunny. Once escrow closed, Joan and her lover Bernard moved in and saw that Bunny had been allowed to get away with murder. Joan put him to work carrying water, whereupon he fell and claimed workmen's comp. "Work through the pain," Joan advised, telling Bernard to motivate Bunny with a good beating.

The malicious little rabbit then fell seriously ill. At the end of her patience, Joan threw him into the street. Once Bunny was on the mend, he tried to return to Joan's house of hookers, but she refused to negotiate. Mr. Bunny then took the matter to court—but got outfoxed. Instead of getting his job back with perks, the presiding judge gave Bunny his freedom to hop away from it all.

IN BONDAGE TO A BAD POET

Busier than a two-career car-pooler with three kids, **La Grosse Margot** was one of many women in fifteenth-century Paris who sold her flesh—along with other soft goods, like tapestry and *other* women's flesh—to make ends meet. But it wasn't all income. She had overhead, too—his name was Francois Villon. Margot, who ran a brothel immodestly close to Notre Dame Cathedral, was but one of Francois' ladies. Not every Paris flesh-flasher had a pimp as cultured as Francois; when he wasn't collecting the panderer's percent, or dealing out corporal punishment to keep a hooker in line, Villon wrote verses, as profane as Paris' meaner streets. In his poem called "Grand Testament," he immortalized Margot (whose handle meant "stout Margie") as well as other hard-working entrepreneurs in his playboy collection, from Blanche the cobbler to Catherine the purse seller. We don't know how stout Margie spent her later years. Villon, however, murdered a priest, appeared on police blotters with regularity, and served time, including ten years' exile. Judging by the literary evidence, Francois shoulda had the book thrown at him for his poetry as well.

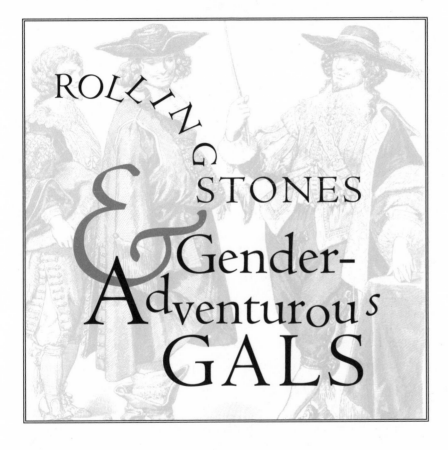

ROLLING STONES & Gender-Adventurous GALS

TAX PROTESTERS & OTHER
TESTY TRANS-AMAZONS

In the Essex town of Maldon, weaving just didn't pay the way it used to, thought English spinsters of both sexes. With their take-home pay, weavers like **Alice Clark** couldn't even buy grain to make bread. In 1629, things got really ugly when the weavers decided they weren't going to take it anymore—and Alice presented herself as a candidate for riot leader. Besides deft fingers and a mean warp and woof, Alice had talents as a cross-dresser and preferred to call herself "Captain." At her urging, the male weavers in the group dressed as women, leaving her to wear the sole codpiece in the crowd. Captain Alice was superb—and the successful grain riot was talked about for years.

Actually, female-led mobs and rioters were veddy old hat in England by then. As early as 1386, **Agnes Sadeler** had raised hackles as the head of an unruly peasant throng of Worchestershire grain rioters. In 1603, over two hundred Lincolnshire women triumphed against a local decision to drain the fen that watered their cattle (all it took was a canal-creaming and a decapitation threat or two). A later generation of female rioters resisted attempts to enclose their lands, using scythes and pitchforks in pointed protest.

Writings of the time reflected this belligerence. A must-read English publication of the day was written by a saucy pseudonymic duo who called themselves "Mary Tattle-Well and Joane Hit-Him-Home, Spinsters." One of their better lines read: "As to the most part of women being liars—it is only out of their goodnesses to cover the faults and abuses of men."

Female protests on a variety of issues in England continued to grow. In 1642, a political protest led by **Anne Stagge** drew four hundred women to present a petition of financial grievances to the Houses of Lords and Commons. Eleven years later, some three thousand women took to the streets to petition for better economic conditions—which, unsurprisingly, had not yet been met—and got knocked heads and a few casualties for their pains.

Popular protests by women, with and without cross-dressing, weren't confined to England. The mid-1600s saw a tax revolt in Montpellier, France, whose chief rabble-rouser was a sturdy woman nicknamed **La Branlaire,** who wore the pants in the family. Similar organized protests and riots on economic and religious issues drew hundreds (and sometimes greater numbers) of women in Italy, Germany, and Spain.

Is the big rake really "me"?

ADVENTURES (AND FELONIES) TO TOP QUIXOTE

 bride at seven, **Leonor López de Córdoba** barely had time to gloat over her wedding gifts (the loot included five hundred Moorish slaves, forty skeins of pearls "as fat as chickpeas," and several kilos of gems) before becoming a political prisoner at age eight.

That's what comes of being a blueblood on the wrong side of a Spanish civil war. Before being clapped in toddler-sized irons, Leonor was treated to the spectacle of her father's head hitting the cobblestones of Plaza de San Francisco in Sevilla. Then she and her twenty-year-old bridegroom, Ruy Gutierrez, plus assorted in-laws, and her favorite brother, Lope, began a nine-year prison stint.

In her autobiography, Leonor recalled those years: "Our husbands had sixty pounds of iron on their feet, and my brother Lope had a chain on top of the irons." Under those merry conditions, it was almost a relief when the plague hit, taking most of Leonor's brothers, sisters, and in-laws.

In 1406, Death made a house call on the king who'd locked them up; his will freed the surviving family. The teen zestfully headed for court, where she became the close personal friend of Catherine, the new ruler of Castile. Those were the glory years: nobody got to see the monarch without going through Leonor's turnstile.

Meanwhile, Leonor's husband tried—and failed—to reclaim his property. Humiliated, he set off to wander the world for seven years, the standard therapy to shore up masculine self-esteem in that era. When he finally showed up, worse for wear and riding a mule, Leonor had been banished from court and was living off the charity of an aunt in Córdoba.

One day, as Leonor and Ruy slunk in for dinner, a servant snickered at them. Status-conscious Leonor got into a high dudgeon—and strangled the slave bare-handed. (Prison had made her testy; besides, in her eyes, it wasn't really homicide—just slave-icide.)

Still, auntie was miffed. To make amends, Leonor took in an orphan who had been scooped up in a raid on the Jewish quarter, baptizing the tad to make a

The cat-o'-nine-tails smarted, but what really hurt was that jailhouse dunce cap.

Christian out of him. This act of "charity" did the trick; Leonor then persuaded auntie to buy property mysteriously "liberated" in the anti-Jewish raid and give it to her. By the time Leonor hit her thirties, she had a couple of palaces, a garden, and some shacks for the servants built on the land.

Just when things were going pretty well, Spain got hit by more years of plagues. Leonor and her family fled the city, but epidemics followed them to her cousin's. After most of her relatives dropped like Spanish flies, Leonor moped back to Córdoba, where she lived to write an autobiography that itself has survived nearly six hundred years.

real guts,
make-believe scrotum

ot many Ren soldiers got gravestones—much less one that read, as **Trijntje Simon**'s did, "Such brave deeds by a woman should not be forgotten, but are worthy of being lodged in the hearts and minds of the Dutch people." Her dad put up the marker for his daughter, who'd spent her adult life passing as "Simon Poort."

Apparently more a male in a female body than a cross-dresser, Trijntje worked as a shoemaker and stonemason in her native land. When military life called, this patriot answered. After a career marked by courage, Trijntje died in battle. Only when her uniform was removed did stupefied officers discover that trooper Poort had balls only in a metaphorical sense. All agreed, however, that whichever latrine he/she had patronized, Poort was a standout. Besides the memorial erected by the elder Simon, a crowd of army officers, naval commanders, and civilian bigwigs attended Trijntje Simon's funeral ceremony at the garrison town of Rees, where she was accorded full military honors.

The Crying Game,
Put to Music

Although newspapers started appearing in Ren times, the big mass-market media in the 1600s was the popular song. When a hero or a rogue like **Trijn Jurriaens** became a household word, publishers would scramble to create a ballad about his or her life. Usually printed on a flyer or broadside, sometimes crudely illustrated, the song (sung to some popular tune) would recount the deeds and misdeeds of a given do-gooder or do-badder. Cheap and easy to read, such ballads sold in huge numbers.

Trijn Jurriaens, a today-male, tomorrow-female swindler, forger, and smooth talker, had more than one popular song written about her—which goes to show how gossip-worthy her tale was. A native of Hamburg, Germany, Trijn plied various illegal trades around Europe under her own name and as "Hendrik Brughman." It was as Hendrik that she courted and bedded another woman, whose delightful naiveté failed to notice her man's lack of equipment for the job. Thrilled nonetheless, the new fiancée laid gifts—maybe even an advance on her dowry money—on Hendrik.

Then, citing "business to attend to back in Hamburg," Hendrik staged a fake farewell at the harbor, changing genders with a dress and a good foundation garment once the fiancée was out of sight.

Trijn's most sung-about coup came years later, however. In 1679, she happened to be at the deathbed of a dear old dame she knew, who gargled that she was leaving her money to the church. Thrifty Trijn just hated to see funds wasted like that. With the help of a female partner in crime, she quickly hid the corpse and stepped in, subbing as the sickabed senior.

Meanwhile, the accomplice rounded up a notary, who came to take down the "deathbed" will of the moribund woman, the new and improved beneficiaries being Trijn and company.

Despite her orderly German background, Trijn was sloppy somewhere along the line; perhaps the body of the deceased started smelling before the check cleared. At any rate, her fraud came to light and Jurriaens served two years in prison. Puzzlingly, as part of her sentence, she had to wear her by-now rather nasty male clothing.

About ten minutes after getting out of the clink, incorrigible Jurriaens was back to committing felonies and misdemeanors. But you could hardly blame her for one of her infractions—stealing a wicker basket of linen. After twenty-four months in jail, you'd long for clean underwear, too.

PLAYFUL ADVENTURER

From debtors' prison to deafening applause as the first female playwright to get her works on England's version of Broadway, **Aphra Amis Behn** came a long way, baby. Her story began in Suriname, of all places, where Aphra spent her youth in the sticky tropics of South America. Eventually she married a Mr. Behn and the couple headed for London in 1665—jolly bad timing, given it was the year of the Great Plague. Behn promptly expired, leaving Aphra unmerry and broke.

Resume in hand, Aphra hit up King Charles of England (who had a small war going with the Dutch) for an espionage job. Delighted, the king sent her to Holland, where bilingual Behn uncovered a plot: the Dutch planned to sail up the Thames and set fire to the English fleet! Well, isn't that *special*, said the king—and failed to heed (or pay) her.

Aphra was starting to get down on men as providers or employers. To finish her spy assignment, what could she do but borrow money for expenses? On her return to London, agent Behn got grim news: not only did the damned Brits refuse to cover her costs—she got tossed in debtors' prison by her creditor! She did get an "I told you so" out of the deal; in June 1667, seventeen Dutch warships attacked an unprepared England, making King Charles the laughingstock of Europe.

Now rotting away in a festering hole, Mrs. B. rethought her career goals. By the time she got released, she had her first risqué play roughed out. By 1670, audiences were splitting their sides over her witty works. Lines like "Come away! Poverty's catching!" made her famous.

Besides her twenty plays, Aphra composed poetry, wrote fourteen novels, and did translations into French (with a time-out here and there for a liaison, one of which came with a bonus of syphilis). Hailed as the first woman in England to earn a living by writing, she was also the first English author to express sympathy for slaves. In one of her books, this racy Renaissance role model defined herself by saying, "I had rather die in the adventure of noble achievements, than live in obscure and sluggish security." In her fifty far-from-sluggish years, Aphra won honors and left a wealth of writings (if not money). She was buried in prestigious Westminster Abbey—but in the actresses' section, rather than her rightful place in Poet's Corner.

If I survive these downers, they'll make a damn good play!

uick—who was Germany's most gender-independent rascal? It could very well have been **Isabella Geelvinck,** a talented cross-dresser who hailed from Bodensee. Even as a youngster in the 1640s, Isabella dug the boots-and-codpiece look—very verboten to her horrified parents. With an "I don't give a furschlugginer," Geelvinck ran away and joined the army, serving as a trooper for five years, then donning a cook's apron for ten more.

This fetishist just could not get her fill of male uniforms. When she mustered out of the service, Isabella headed for Holland and became a gentleman's valet in the town of Amersfoort. Too dull by half, she thought, and left, lifting a substantial amount of silver and linen from her employer as a memento. She had luggage by now, so it wasn't hard to slip into something more comfortable (and feminine) to escape the hue and cry behind her.

Once in the Dutch city of Utrecht, Isabella decided to try domestic service from the distaff side, hiring on as a maid. She quickly found that this gig was even duller and tougher than being a manservant. Although adept at cross-dressing (and undressing), Geerlinck didn't have much talent for successful theft. Inevitably, her female employer caught her pilfering. Instead of saying, "You're canned and outta here!" the mistress of the house tried to, you know, rehabilitate Isabella. After recounting the forks, she told the light-fingered maid, "We're gonna put this all behind us—I'll even let you finish out your work contract. Now get cracking on that privy cleanup!"

Touched by her mistress' concern, Isabella dutifully completed her contracted time. Wanting to make a memorable "Goodbye!" gesture, she then set the house on fire. As maladroit at arson as she was at petty theft, Isabella Geelvinck got caught. By now, Dutch authorities had pretty much given up on Isabella's possibilities as a productive member of society—*any* society. Still, the sentence they handed down must have given Geelvinck a big gulp: death by strangulation.

thinker, tailor, doctor, spy

Baptized **Anne Murray,** she was a middle-class English girl whose sharp mind and passion for life didn't make up for her major fault: a glaring dowry deficiency in the polite but mercenary society she lived in. (Her inheritance was tied up in a legal battle.)

To make matters worse, Anne had fallen hard for Thomas Howard, who really needed to marry someone who was loaded. Gallant Tom wanted to run away and wed Anne secretly, but she refused, being no slouch at chivalry herself.

At length, Anne got a new suitor, someone calling himself Colonel Bampfylde. He claimed to be unmarried, thus overcoming Anne's qualms about rolls in the hay. Lying came naturally; he was a double (possibly triple) agent—and this was wartime. About 1647, he asked Anne to help with some top-level spy stuff. Their mission? To rescue hulking young James, the duke of York, from his house arrest at St. James' Palace.

Anne's assignment—to disguise the duke in a female getup—taxed her persuasive powers to the utmost. Tailor after tailor shuddered at the measurements she brought in ("You want that? In *mohair*?") At length, outsized garments in hand, Miss Braveheart and the duke rendezvoused near London Bridge, where she promptly out-fitted him. With his long curls and girlish face, he made quite a babe. (In her memoirs, Anne recalled him as "very pretty.")

With her help, the duke escaped to join his sister in Holland. That was merely the first of Murray's adventures, however. Alone, Anne made her way to Scotland, spending two years on the battle-field, treating maggoty, gangrene-laden soldiers with balsams and medicines she'd brought from England. She soon was drafted as a midwife and a doctor to the Scottish Army (given the weather and their "all the haggis you can eat" policies, they were lucky to get any-body, much less the sterling Miss Murray).

When the conflict ended, ever-flexible Anne took a job as gov-erness in the household of Sir James Halkett. He was a Scottish wid-ower; she was single. It looked like a perfect match. Anne's dowry, however, was still hung up in court. Meanwhile, her fabricating old flame showed up, still talking trash about not being married, and wouldn't she fancy a bit of the Bampfylde bump again.

This time around, Anne wasn't having any. She turned down the Colonel's proposition, and accepted that of James. Now thirty-three, she was ready to leave the single life and embark on a marital adven-ture as Lady Anne Halkett. What's more, she had the time to leave behind the fascinating diary of her life.

ROADS SCHOLAR

oached by her erudite father Fulvio, **Olimpia Morata** and her gigabyte intellect came to the plush Italian court of Ferrara, growing up in the spotlight as the trick pony of the court. Her best pal was Anne, daughter of Duchess Renée, Head Mozzarella of the Ferrara court. The two girls studied together, tutored by a German humanist. In no time, Olimpia had a mature understanding of Latin, Greek, and the humanities; for kicks, she wrote essays, letters, poems, and dialogues. She opted not to study religion formally, but pored over the Old and New Testaments on her own.

In 1542, when she was sixteen, the larger world of religious conflict came into her life. With Protestant groups springing up everywhere, Catholic officials fired up a Roman Inquisition. In this hysterical atmosphere, intellectuals were pressed to declare their sympathies. Along with her dad, her tutor, and some German friends, Olimpia was part of a circle intent on religious reform. Once the court hotshots, they all fell into disgrace. When her dad died in 1548, Olimpia even got booted out of Ferrara. Talk about petty: the duchess made her return the fancy duds she'd worn there. (Still, wardrobe removal was better than being asked to don the *sanbenito*— the garment worn en route to a heretic's bonfire.)

In 1550, Olimpia married Dr. Andreas Grunthler, a Lutheran she'd gotten to know and love at Ferrara, and the two beat it for Germany. Once at Schweinfurt, the new bride got into the fledgling Protestant cause. A one-woman PR firm for Lutheranism and for religious tolerance, she wrote incessantly to friends, rulers, and fellow exiles.

While eloquent, her peace pleas were hopeless. War began to roll over Europe. When Schweinfurt was besieged, she and Andreas fled. The very first day, they were attacked by bandits; crabby because Olimpia had a zero balance in her ransom contingency fund, they took her husband hostage. The following day, a second set of less fussy ruffians stole her clothes and shoes.

Stressed out and barefoot, she fell ill with malaria. Over time, valiant Morata pulled herself together, won her husband's release, and even finagled the guy a teaching job at the University of Heidelberg. But by then, Olimpia had had about all she could take. At twenty-nine, she quit this Earth. Instead of a nice casket, her last request to Andreas was to publish the scraps of her writing that she'd been able to reconstruct. One lovely fragment says: "Remembering that the span of our life is but toil and trouble and we soon fly away, may I give myself to the contemplation of things eternal."

THE WORLD WAS HER OYSTER

Who says Ren royal women were stay-at-homes? In globe-trotting, some of them out-Dianaed our twentieth-century Diana. **Mary of Hungary** (who also liked to be called "the Diana" for her goddesslike hunting and riding abilities) grew up in Austria and Germany, got married in France, spent seven years as queen of Hungary, then worked for twenty years as the regent of the Netherlands, pro temming for her brother Charlie. (The rest of the world knew him as Charles V, Holy Roman Emperor.)

As a young Hapsburg royal like Charlie, Mary's first assignment was to learn how to spend money. Lots of it. Married at sixteen to teenaged King Louis of Hungary, she began her fiscal training by dropping one-third of the annual income of Hungary and Bohemia on her showy court—a move which angered local nobles terribly, who felt that those coffers were *theirs* to suck dry.

Mary ignored their petty grumblings. In 1526, her attention turned elsewhere. After an unfortunate war in which a massively unprepared Hungarian armed force, led by young Louie, was ground into the dirt by a bunch of Turks, Mary became a widow. She hung around Hungary just long enough to see her younger brother on the throne, then got her new assignment: to run the Netherlands as its regent. Ever the trouper, Mary womanfully took over the reins and began to suck the Dutch coffers dry.

She was a great hostess—her dinners were famous. Naturally, everyone who dined with her wanted to impress her in return, to show their own lavish profligacy. One well-intentioned host, newly rich but not too couth, planned a dazzler of a dinner. To out-Hapsburg a Hapsburg, he had every single one of the oyster appetizers gold-plated. (Talk about a groaning table.)

But life wasn't just the world's most expensive canapés. Ever since her brother Charlie had become Holy Roman Emperor, a team of protesters headed by Martin Luther had been lining up for a Protestant–Catholic Superbowl. Since Mary had military moxie and aggression to spare, she played on the Emperor's team, winning several wars in the Netherlands-versus-France playoffs. Her greatest triumph? An end run into Picardy, where her troops burned down seven hundred French villages. That time, the oysters were blackened, not gold-plated.

FIGHTING FEMME—
UNTIL THE LAST FRAME

n English folk hero or heroine, depending on the situation, **Long Meg** hitchhiked a ride on a carrier's cart from her native Lancashire, heading for London town to make a life for herself—one that seesawed between male and female roles.

Her first gig was as an attractive (albeit very tall) serving maid in a local tavern, where she was soon raking in good tips from the oh-so-friendly soldier clientele. It wasn't long before Meg had to show her mettle rather than her cleavage. In one incident, she stepped in to keep some army buddies from being robbed. Soon, however, stories circulated about Long Meg's penchant for putting on breeches and fightintg ale-enhanced locals in duels.

At length, her winning way with a sword emboldened Meg to take on an obnoxious swell who called himself James of Castile. After dusting Sir James, she rubbed in the victory by making him act as her "serving wench" and bring her supper. Then Meg revealed her own wenchly qualities to give the Sir further humiliation.

On another occasion, Long Meg took on a job as a washer-woman for English troops in France. When an enemy soldier got too mouthy, she pinned him in two outta three, then gave him the old *Voilà! Je suis femme!* routine.

Long Meg never tired of the outrageous fun of cross-dressing. For a time, she owned a tavern in Islington; when an unruly patron jumped one of her barmaids, she whipped the tar out of him with a cudgel (a club and the favored weapon of sixteenth-century English streetfighting), then staged an impromptu parade through the streets—him in a barmaid's getup, her strutting in breeches and doublet.

This bawdy brawler left lots of legends but no memoirs; however, a male writer with a nose for what sells jumped into the breech, as it were. In 1582, a chapbook (the forerunner of our beach paperback) called *Long Meg of Westminster* made its debut. His yarn ended with a crowd-pleasing twist for the heavily male readership of the day: in the final chapter, this Amazonian cross-dresser marries a soldier and simpers, "It behoveth me to be Obedient to you. Even if I Cudgel a Knave, never let it be said that Long Meg shall be her Husband's Master." However bogus the behoveth ending, the story of Long Meg continued to fascinate; four more book versions (and countless popular songs) of her life appeared between 1620 and 1690.

DOING IT DECIDEDLY HER WAY

 tall blonde with brains and backtalk, **Kristina of Sweden** had a way with a rifle, an addiction to army vittles, and an aversion to combs. Hey, you'd be eccentric too, if your nutsy mom had made you mourn your kingly father by hanging his pickled heart in a gold casket above your black velvet-draped bed.

When mom finally went for a long rest in the country, Kris got an education (and a wardrobe) fit for a king. She learned to ride the most spirited horses and use lethal weapons. Her tutors piled on the homework, math to foreign languages. What with her hours in the saddle and her class load, there wasn't much time for sleeping. No problem. This gigabyte intellect thrived on five hours a night. Kris wanted to be like her military daddy—so she kept her rooms icy cold and lived on rations of salt herring, bread, and cheese.

In 1644, this ink-stained teen became queen of Sweden. Still refusing to comb her dreaded locks, she wore stylish male headgear to inspect warships and receive guests. Kristina's caffeinated brilliance required sparring partners of equal intellect. To make her court a Camelot of the North, she invited big-name brains, scoring a coup when French genius René Descartes agreed to an autumn visit. The queenly fresh-air fiend kept Descartes hopping—but not warm. In

January, he died of lung congestion. Instantly Sweden fell into last place as a fun destination.

Although her rebellious heart wasn't in it, Kristina reigned for twenty-two years, expanding Swedish industry and being a dutiful Lutheran. She also reduced the treasury to Jenny Craig size by creating 450 new nobles, whom she then had to support.

In 1654, she abdicated in favor of her cousin Charles Gustave, then made her way to Rome to become a private citizen—and a Catholic. Before long, she gave an "It's a new pope!" bash for her good buddy, Clement IX. A memorable affair—too memorable, perhaps. After drunken guests began to riot, Kris showed how to shut a party down by ordering her guards to fire on the crowd. Eight bodies later, that party was definitely *over.*

The seventeenth century had its own Funny Girl.

But Kris' lifestyle of murderous events, celebrity friends, and art collecting just didn't cut it, profundity-wise. Over the years, she tried Lutheranism, lesbianism, Catholicism, and a throne-grab or two in Poland and Naples; likewise, nada. When she died at sixty-three, the restless Swede with a mind as quick as mercury had become just another of Rome's fabulous local characters.

BEING ALL
THAT SHE COULD BE

rawn by the "Now hiring! Entry level!" signs, small-town **Maritgen Jens,** the fifteen-year-old daughter of a defunct gunsmith, hit the cobblestones of Amsterdam, only to find that *entry level* meant "pittance" (a word originally coined to describe the daily food allowance of a monk). Her job making silk thread was OK, but advancement was nil. And that special "female pittance" pay? The pits. Unwilling to give up, Maritgen sold her clothes, used her laughable paycheck to get some male attire, called herself David, and applied for work at a silk thread joint down the road. Hired at male wages this time, soon Maritgen was bobbin' right along. As David, she made foreman—and unbeknownst to the boss, became the establishment's first female in middle management.

But Jens sought larger horizons. Once she looked old enough, she enlisted in the Dutch army and got sent to Africa. She could spit shine, double time, and soldier as well as any man, but then Jens fell ill. At the hospital, she got overexposed—then exposed (those darned hospital gowns!). The local governor gave Maritgen an ultimatum: Return to Holland, or marry a local. The guv, who had exquisite taste in women's clothing, lined up a gown and jewelry for Jens. Then he put out a call for groom candidates, who visited the cross-dresser on the mend to show their best bedside manners. Maritzen chose a thirtysomething legal professional; three weeks later, she was a bride. Heavily invested in this whole affair, the guv paid for a four-day nuptial blowout and even gave away the bride.

Sad to relate, Maritgen's groom didn't take to marriage. Sexual incompatibility? More like climate incompatibility. He succumbed to a nasty tropical ailment, and before long, the new widow was on a slow boat headed back to Holland. On the bright side, this time Maritgen had an army pension—plus a male *and* a female wardrobe.

COMING OUT
OF THE ARMOIRE

Because of anti-sodomy laws making lesbianism as felonious as intimacy with barnyard animals, there just weren't that many "I'm out!" parties in Renaissance centuries, even in oh-so-erotic France.

So the public actions of **Aubigny de Maupin**—to say nothing of what she did behind closed doors—furnished considerable fuel for outrage in the late 1600s. Born poor, the beauteous Aubigny clawed her way out of the Parisian gutter into the French Opera, becoming a contralto singer. Equally marvelous was her way with a sword—no doubt a useful skill when you're clawing your way out of the gutter.

After a performance, there was nothing that Mlle. de Maupin liked better than to throw on her favorite leisure wear—that of a fashionable French cavalier—and go kick some serious male derrière in a back alley. In her most notorious duel, she took on three male opponents who'd gotten riled when she passionately kissed "their" girl on the dance floor. Interrupted in mid-osculation, Maupin puffed out her chest and said, "You wanna piece a me? Hanh?" Depending on whose version you believe, she either dispatched the trio or killed them. Since dueling was a felony within the city limits, she could have been in *très* deep trouble; but the king was amused by Maupin's masquerade, and let her off.

On stage, Aubigny often took male roles, and used her dueling abilities. So rapid was her rapier that audiences found it hard to believe Aubigny was female; on one occasion, she had to go topless temporarily to prove it.

A woman of great passions, she dazzled and won a variety of females. One piquant caper was her runaway affair with a nun from

Ze women, zey go mad for my fake goatee—touché!

Avignon, who crawled back to her convent, utterly spent, three months later. That little stunt earned Aubigny a felony sentence, which was later commuted, of being burnt at the stake. But Miss de Maupin kept on pushing the outrage envelope. While on tour in Marseilles, her masterful performance as a male cavalier stunned a young fan, who ran off with her post-opera. This episode probably wouldn't have attracted that much notice, except the fan was a fat-cat merchant's daughter. To avoid a lesbian/anti-sodomy bonfire, the runaway later claimed to have blown the whistle on Maupin "just as soon as I discovered her gender, your honor."

On this charge, Aubigny went to jail and had a prime seat on death row. Luckily, audiences in Paris and elsewhere fancied the diva so much that public clamor overturned her sentence. From that point on, jaded authorities said, *"C'est la vie"* to Maupin's subsequent high jinks, no matter how flamboyant or outré.

shape-shifter

 t didn't take June or moon to make **Cornelia Croon**—just money, and a pair of male breeches with a matching doublet. A Dutch maid who made a living from bogus life insurance annuities, she cashed in her forged artwork as Cornelia, then left town decked out as Cornelius. Neat trick, since the Groningen authorities invariably put out a "wanted" poster for a female. At the apogee of her career, Cornelia even shared "most wanted" honors with three killers, when her mug shot ran in Holland's largest newspaper, the *Haarlemmer Courant.*

What tripped up the tricky Crooner? In a word, kids. Not hers—the ones she robbed. Seems that Cornelia took up a mugging minors when she hit Amsterdam. (That city's youth must have been as affluent as today's young arcade-goers.) Busted while in male duds, she received a once-over from suspicious doctors and a grilling from police—at which time, twisty Cornelia's true curves came to light.

Naturally the officials in Groningen wanted a piece of the action, and had her extradited. Of all the rotten luck: in the late 1670s, Cornelia got sentenced to hang for paper-hanging and kid-swindling. Fortunately, a tender-hearted magistrate commuted her necktie party to banishment for ninety years. Where the clothes-happy Croon spent her remaining decades, and how, remains a mystery.

BRITAIN'S FIRST
ROLLING STONE

spa aficionada before the words "pamper package" had even been dreamed up, **Celia Fiennes** kept detailed notes of her wanderings through every county in England, which eventually grew into *The Journeys of Celia Fiennes*. A lady of leisure, she probably began the writing—like her travels—as a lark. But Celia, who certainly rates as one of England's early travel eccentrics, chronicled eighteen years of travel—and made at least 13,000 miles of her adventures from the back of a horse.

Born at Banbury Castle in 1662 to a family of jumped-up society folks, Miss Fiennes dabbled at being a lady-in-waiting but was bored out of her gourd. Fortunately, a sharp attack of hypochondria hit, and the twenty-three-year-old decided to do a circuit of English "spaws" to take the waters. Celia became hooked on H_2O, the smellier the better. As she vagabonded, first to improve her health, her interests widened.

An early Kurault of the British Isles, the lifelong Miss Fiennes explored coal mines and caves, mingled with artisans and religious dissenters, popped in on the queen and her court at Hampton Court, and got down in the dirt on archaeological sites.

Although she often stayed with relatives or friends, Celia traveled rough. Accompanied by one or two servants, she attended beer tastings, survived falls with her horse, and eluded road bandits with equal élan. On her longest single journey in 1697, she covered six hundred miles in six weeks. Her exploits, it's said, even got her immortalized in a familiar nursery rhyme:

> Ride a cock horse to Banbury Cross
> To see a fine lady upon a white horse.
> Rings on her fingers, and bells on her toes
> She shall have music, wherever she goes.

Written in breathless prose, with heavy reliance on descriptors like "neat," Celia's book was not great literature. Instead, she gave a priceless and thorough look at a natural landscape and a society that was growing in material prosperity. Firsthand in every particular, and with no hidden agenda or patron to please, Celia's writings still reflect the quirky and unquenchable curiosity of an astonishingly independent woman who pleased herself first as she rambled about England. Who says that rolling stones have to be British males?

why they called it
"the age of discovery"

 muchacha of modest means from a Spanish burg, **Elena de Céspedes** wed at sixteen, got pregnant, and was promptly abandoned. Once her son was born, Elena left him with Mom and headed for Granada. A big change, she sensed, was in the air.

Or under her clothing. Under those voluminous skirts, Elena discovered she now had an organ requiring a codpiece cover! Armed with this knowledge, she began an affair with her landlord's wife, who seemed anxious to explore this new frontier with Eleno, as she took to calling her/himself. Our gender-challenged protagonist soon learned to brag about her sexual prowess, leave the toilet lid up, and other critical male skills—and then it was off to the army.

After a couple of tours of duty, this sixteenth-century Pretender left for Madrid to become a tailor. Again fortunate in her lodging choices, nimble Eleno rented from a surgeon who taught her how to cut hair, let blood, and amputate without anesthetic. Granted, the local ER scene was exciting, but restless Céspedes tired of it. She went back to village life—where she fell deeply in love.

This time around, Eleno got permission to marry the girl. The pair made a quick trip to Madrid for a priest's OK, who doubtfully looked at Eleno's hairless face and said, "Are you a eunuch?"

Bureaucracy. To get a marriage license, Eleno had to pay for a front and back inspection by doctors, who duly noted her matching set of male organs. The sweethearts married—but more cowpies littered to path to true happiness. They moved to a town with no surgeon, so Eleno could set up shop. Unfortunately, its mayor had been in Eleno's army unit and remembered something odd about him. Soon charges were brought: impersonating a man, and/or mocking the sacrament of marriage.

The same team of doctors came to reinspect Eleno. After a double take, they said: Better put out an all-points bulletin—Eleno's male organs were definitely missing. There was, however, a vagina. "Must be the devil's work," they surmised. In his/her defense, Eleno said that he/she was a hermaphrodite, "but I had cancer, and the male parts dropped off." This didn't play well with the authorities, who turned the whole diabolical mess over to the Spanish Inquisition. Unless you were in league with the devil, sex changes (and changebacks) were impossible, they thundered.

Innocent of anything other than possession of male and female organs that appeared and disappeared with disconcerting abandon, Eleno nevertheless was convicted. His/her punishment? Two hundred lashes at a public whipping—followed by ten years in a public hospital, where Céspedes found serenity, but darned little freedom.

OFF AGAIN, ON AGAIN SOLDIER

he odyssey (some might say "odd-essy") of **Christian Davies** began one evening when her husband Richard Welch failed to come home from a Dublin tavern. Twelve months later, Richard wrote to say he'd gotten trashed that night, been shanghaied to France, then forced to sign on with the army to earn money to get back. Uh-huh. His note failed to include a return address.

A physically fit type who didn't fancy waiting for an errant husband to find his way home, Chris stashed her two kids with her mother and set off to join the service. After donning her husband's suit, she got herself a good wig, hat, sword, and was signed up as "Christopher" Welch, no problem. First stop, Holland, where Chris got shot, taken prisoner, then exchanged for a French POW—passing muster even under those trying conditions. Feeling sorta macho, Chris went after an NCO for attacking a girl. "The brig for you, soldier!" was the next thing she heard. Talk about privacy issues—jail was the worst. Fortunately, Chris traveled with a piece of equipment she'd gotten from another fem in camouflage that let her urinate standing up. Soon she got a pardon and was sprung, with no one the wiser.

By 1692, she'd joined another regiment, participating in the successful siege of Namurs. Time for a bit of R and R, she thought, and tooled over to Ireland to check on her children. All being quiet on the western front, she sailed to Holland to reenlist.

By now a somewhat grimy vet, Chris finally caught sight of her husband on a battlefield. Shock! Joy! A rendezvous—marred a tad by a Dutch gal in high-heel clogs who said, "I'm his wife," which Richard disputed. Chris didn't care; by now, she had a thing for army life as a male. The Welches became dogface buddies, fighting side by side, until that fateful day when Chris got a skull fracture from an incoming round.

This time, less lackadaisical surgeons actually examined her body and discovered parts to Chris that made her a Christine. The commanding officer took it very well. After Richard confessed, "That was no brother, that was my wife," the commander ordered, "You officers—chip in and buy her some decent dresses!" He started the ball rolling by giving her a new silk gown himself, then added new duty assignments as cook, courier, and nurse.

Unthrilled to be out of the action, Chris nevertheless stuck with the army until Richard bought it in battle, then returned to the Emerald Isle. With her army pension, she opened a tavern and pie house in Dublin, which she ran for decades. Chris mellowed over the years. At times, she even got wild and crazy and threw on a dress, earning the nickname "Mother Ross." The year she turned 108, she died at Chelsea Hospital and was buried with military honors—a soldier to the last.

PATRON SAINT
OF AVON

 careerwoman with calves of iron, **Joan Dant** pioneered the door-to-door sales pitch in seventeenth-century England. Her peddler prowess became famous in London and environs—where working conditions included grouchy dogs, no sidewalks, filthy cobblestones, and flying chamberpots.

Only after becoming a weaver's widow did Mrs. Dant decide to become a traveling entrepreneur. She started with socks, then built up her inventory to carry a whole line of hosiery and haberdashery.

A Quaker by faith, the honesty of her business dealings—and the great networking she did among fellow Quakers—soon made Joan Dant the peddler to watch. In time, Dant enterprises went international. Modest by nature, and a thrift queen at heart, Joan schlepped her wares to faraway Paris and Brussels, all the while amassing the Renaissance equivalent of money market funds.

Thanks to her daily cardiovascular workouts, she didn't perish until age eighty-four. At that time, sorrowing friends and startled beneficiaries found that the dauntless marathon miler was worth a small fortune. Most of the 9,000 pounds and other assets she left went to Quaker widows and fatherless children. As Joan put it, "I got it by the rich and I mean to leave it to the poor."

Slick **T**ALKERS **&** *A w e s o m e* NETWORKERS

OWNED BY A POSTAL JONES

In 1619, **Sarel Gutman** became cofounder of what may have been the world's first private postal service. The new postmistress and her husband Loeb had picked the right demographic: the literate residents of the Prague Ghetto, a Jewish enclave in Bohemia's capital city and one of the biggest in Europe.

Why did Sarel and her husband attempt to get this novel idea (heretofore the preserve of rulers, rich people, and the military) off the ground? It wasn't a good time to launch any business—besides the usual plagues and riots, the Thirty Years' War was about to begin. Maybe the Gutmans were trying to keep the lines of communication open in their marriage. Loeb often went to Vienna and other cities to seek work, leaving Sarel and the kids hundreds of miles away.

Once the entrepreneurs had fired a few trial letters back and forth, they thought, "Why not give this concept the full Monty?" Sarel and Loeb passed the word about their new postal priorities, and in short order, they had their hands full. Of mail. The threat of war, job shortages, and other events meant that countless ghetto dwellers had long-distance relationships, just like the Gutmans. Instead of sitting home worrying, now they could reach out and kvetch!

Aware they were on to something, the couple worked out a schedule of charges, based on length of letter. On the Prague end, .

Sarel distributed letters, collected fees, and sent lists of paid customers to Loeb. To make ends meet, Mrs. Gutman also had to find venture capital, borrowing money at high interest rates.

There was a darker side to the Gutman's brainchild. Sarel got deeply hooked on home delivery. Pretty soon she needed more letters—then more—to feed her habit. As she pleads in one missive to Loeb, "If I did not have two letters a week, I thought that I should not be able to live longer. . . . " Sensitive to charges of favoritism, Sarel and Loeb decided to assess *themselves* the going rate for their letters, too. This penalized Sarel further: "I was very eager to write you, but I was afraid that I should have to pay too great a fee to the messenger, so much have I to write to you."

Wouldn't you know it, politics intervened to cut Sarel off at the height of her addiction. In November 1619 a fancy-schmancy new Protestant king, Frederick I, got crowned in Prague. Two weeks later, the regular run of the Gutman postal service got hit by Austrian troops, the mail sack confiscated. Stuffed somewhere, undelivered, while religious war gradually enveloped all of Europe, the letters sat until their rediscovery in the twentieth century. Today, the heartfelt missives of Sarel and others in the Prague Ghetto can once again be read in all their Yiddish eloquence.

ORANGE GIRL WAS NO LEMON AT STAND-UP

orn in Drury Lane, a London slum that even the gutter-snipes sniffed at, **Nell Gwynn** hawked fish and oysters on street corners. Later, while tending bar in her mom's House O' Ille Repute, she decided to try for a more challenging career: the sought-after gig of orange girl in the pit of Killigrew's Theatre. Oh, to end up a celebrity like the trollops on Dung Wharf!

At thirteen, Nelly got her dream job hawking citrus. With her bawdy banter and beauty, she soon got asked to be an actress. (There were now job ops galore for females in the newly revived, Puritan-free English theater.) Nell was a natural; she could dance, sing, and play comic roles, too. Soon all of London was in love with her pert expression, dark curly hair, milky skin, brilliant blue eyes, and shapely legs, revealed when she danced in her pneumonia-courting short pleated skirt called a Rhinegraves. She and her lover, actor Charles Hart, shot to the top, often playing what were called "gay couple" roles: witty heterosexual lovers with a commitment phobia.

In 1668, she had an after-gig date with a fan in his box. The king himself, Charles II, was having an incognito night out in the next box. Next thing she knew, the king swept Nell and her fan off to a late supper, bringing his brother along to keep the suitor occupied while the king showed the actress his own lines.

When the bill came, both royals fell back on the old "Forgot my wallet" ploy. While the cringing suitor took out a loan to pay the bill, Nell (ever a quick study) said, in a perfect imitation of the king's voice and vocabulary, "Odd's fish, but this is the poorest company I've ever been with at a tavern!"

With that remark, Nell won the king, from heart to gonads. She quickly became his mistress, a relationship that would endure her entire life. Pity that King Charles II wasn't as faithful to her; the drain on English taxpayers would have been substantially less if he'd stuck to one mistress. Or even one gender.

Although she gave the king her loyalty and love, as well as a son who was later made the duke of St. Albans, Nell accepted the revolving door of countesses, actresses, and other lovers in the king's bed. Always puckish, Nell once put on black mourning clothes. When someone asked why, she said, "I'm mourning for the ruined hopes of the duchess of Portsmouth"—a mistress who'd just been replaced by a mightysoft version 9.0.

Pragmatic as only a Cockney can be, Nell took the cash and let the credit go. In fact, when King Charles died, and his brother James took over (no love lost there—Nell called him "dismal Jimmy"), her main worry was her pension. Dismal Jimmy honored it, but cut it in half. Not to worry, guv'ner—spunky Nell managed to survive just fine on her real estate income and annuities until her death in 1687.

PUBLISHING PARAGON

A Parisian with fifty nifty years of publishing and printing books, **Charlotte Guillard** was the nonpareil of literacy in sixteenth-century France. She got her start in this exciting new industry when she married Berthold Rembolt, co-owner of the prestigious Soleil d'Or printing company in Paris. In 1507, the couple took a big plunge: they signed a ninety-nine-year lease on a huge building project. *Beaucoup* bucks later, the couple had a two-unit hotel that housed the Guillards plus their entire roster of workers and families.

Around 1519, Charlotte became a widow, putting her own imprint on the Soleil d'Or books, until husband number two materialized. Was it *l'amour*? Probably propinquity. Claude Chevallon owned a nearby bookstore; with his marriage, he now became a printer-publisher. Charlotte, on the other hand, became invisible, at least to the naked eye. Still an active partner, she signed contracts and paid bills, but disappeared from the "glamour" side of the business.

Sixteen years later, Charlotte's name reappeared as an imprint. A change of heart on Claude's part? More like a change of venue. Now a widow for the second time, Mme. Guillard choked back her grief and took up again as CEO of Soleil d'Or, along with running a busy bookstore. Sans children and meddling mates, she got to do exactly as she pleased for the next twenty years.

She ran four or five presses, employing twelve to twenty-four operators. Likewise, she had a sales force for the bookstore, an accountant to crunch the numbers, and even a couple of cooks—it being customary to feed the help. Charlotte employed other women, too; pay records still exist for her niece **Marye Baugaurd,** possibly an editor or a corrector.

This paragon of publishing profited by an excellent location next to the Catholic Sorbonne University; over the decades, she put out a number of Protestant-ripping books for the professorial crowd. Charlotte also specialized in civil law books, dictionaries, scientific works, and Greek and Latin classics. At times, Guillard went out on a limb to publish projects, notably *Historia Plantarum,* a book that later gained the distinction of being banned by the Sorbonne.

Her greatest contribution was the Greek and Latin dictionary of famed scholar Jacques Toussaint, who'd died leaving a manuscript in four messy clumps. Charlotte had horrendous editorial and technical problems with it. Years later, when she finally got the great work off the press, she wrote a preface, saying: "His most learned lucubrations not only deserved that I should put all the money I had into printing them, but that I should borrow from my friends."

As any sane author would echo, writers had no greater friend than debt-ridden, highly principled Charlotte Guillard—whose Soleil d'Or imprint is still alive and kicking.

169

HER COMET BROUGHT
GIRLS GOOD LUCK

 clear-eyed observer of human foibles, **Bathsua Pell Makin** had no illusions about what men wanted from women—and this diminutive preacher's daughter thought they'd be better off coupling with primates a little further down the old *Time-Life* scale. In her 1673 non-best-seller, Bathsua blasted, "Had God intended women only as a finer sort of cattle, he would not have made them reasonable. Brutes, a few degrees higher than Drils or Monkies might have better fitted some mens' Lust, Pride, and Pleasure; especially those that desire to keep women ignorant to be tyrannized over."

Born in England in 1612, she was the younger sis of gifted linguist and mathematician John Pell, her mentor. (So much for math skills—John ended up in pauper's prison, and she wrote about her visits there with chilling firsthand precision.) Bathsua, however, knew red ink from black. Married briefly to a shadowy nonprovider named Makin, she worked as a professional scholar, governess, and teacher.

With her nonexistent savings, Bathsua eventually traveled to Holland. Her dream? To sit at the knees of Dutch scholarly savant **Anna Maria von Schurmann.** Gouda was great, the tulips lovely, but

Bathsua was really knocked out by the rights that most Dutch women (and not just wealthy geniuses like Anna Maria) enjoyed.

Fired with inspiration, Bathsua began to write books, then opened a school for girls in 1663 at Tottenham High Cross outside London. At first, she had high hopes that a curriculum packed with physics, math, logic, history, and foreign languages would fly. Given the tenor of the times, she soon found she had to dumb down the offerings considerably just to get kids signed up. Her new parent-pandering brochure promised that girls would spend half their time on dancing, music, singing, writing, and keeping accounts—and the balance on electives like languages or hard science. Even with that compromise, her success was a constant battle, but Bathsua kept the school running for at least ten years.

Neither the school nor Bathsua's many writings and books brought her a comfortable livelihood, or even retirement. Bathsua lived into her seventies. Sticky as the wickets got, she never gave up her determination to convince the world of the need for female education.

As the small but supercharged teacher herself noted with a cynical sigh, "A learned woman is thought to be a comet, that bodes mischief whenever it appears."

They Gave Peace a Chance

When's the last time you sent a "Ladies' Peace Day" greeting card, or saw it marked on your calendar? Doesn't ring a bell? Well, join the club. The Ladies' Peace, or *Paix des Dames* (sometimes called the Treaty of Cambrai, if it's referred to at all), however, was a very big deal on August 3, 1529.

On that momentous date, two patrician women met to sign papers. In the blue trunks, representing France, was dowager **Queen Louise of Savoy** (signing on behalf of her young son Francis). In the red knickers was **Margaret of Austria** (signing in for her nephew, Holy Roman Emperor Charles V). The women weren't there as photo ops or mere signature stand-ins. They did the negotiating, hammering out a complex treaty that—among other things—gave parts of Italy its freedom from French domination, and traded two French princes for a pile of Krugerrands. Radical idea, huh: two women working out a peace treaty. Too bad it didn't stick—or set a precedent. The Ladies' Peace lasted about fifteen minutes before France and the Holy Roman Empire engaged in further treacheries and aggressions.

I could kill the guy who got me involved in this peace treaty.

172

GOOSED BY A BREACH OF PROMISE

**gnes Louth** was loath to complain about John Astlott, her steady. But darn it, he was always out of town on business, leaving her chez Louth in York, England. "Dad's getting on my case—propose, or get off the pot," she smartly told John, on the eve of his latest departure for gay Paree or some such place. Upon his return, John had the class to bring a gift goose to soften the old boy up. In the presence of her parents and a large white fowl, the two exchanged betrothal vows, making it official. Then her new fiancé was off again. This time, however, his business went sour. Very sour. When John returned, hoping for some hot kisses and a little commiseration, Agnes yelled, "Whaddaya mean, your net worth is now a goose egg? The wedding's off!" and showed him the door. "Legally, we're already married," John responded. With that, the battle was on, and John took Agnes to court for breach of promise. The issue: Did a lousy goose preempt one of the few rights a Ren woman had—the prerogative to change her mind?

You can stick that ring all right—but not on my finger.

173

home alone can be hell

rench by birth, Huguenot Protestant by religion, royal by lineage, and a real Tartar when the chips were down, **Charlotte de la Trémoille** emerged as the Heroick Countess of the English Civil War. Back when she'd married James Stanley, the earl of Derby and proprietor of the Isle of Man and gobbets of other real estate, Charlotte had merely been thought of as a jolly good catch. In 1642, James was away on the Isle of Man and she'd just put the finishing touches on Lathom House when a messy civil war broke out between the Royalists (who supported the hereditary monarchy) and the Parliamentarians (a power-to-the-people bunch who thought royalty rule was bogus).

Soon, General Fairfax of the no-stinking-royals faction decided to seize Charlotte's spread, and sent a note to the home-alone countess: "Congratulations! Your fabulous home has been selected, out of thousands of candidates, to be besieged by our modest little army. Rather than harm a hair on your exquisitely coiffured head, may we have the pleasure of your timely exit and surrender?"

If Charlotte and her daughters had followed protocol, they could have left without harm. But the countess had plenty of food and water, a well-defended fortress, and a garrison of soldiers. Rather than send back a ringing No!, she wrote that she needed more time "to study his summons" and she "just didn't feel comfortable" meeting outside Lathom House. What with these and other diplomatic sallies, Charlotte delayed the siege for ages.

At length, the general put down his pen and took up arms, pounding her house and matching fortress with mortars, grenades, and cannons. The dust raised made housekeeping incredibly difficult. But the neighbors kicked up even more, leaning on Charlotte to surrender: "It'd be better for the future—our future."

At that point, Countess Charlotte took the offensive, making a dash outside Lathom's walls to snatch away the Big Bertha that had been smacking them with eighty-pound stones day after day. General Fairfax had invited guests ("BYO sand chairs") to witness what he thought would be the torching of Lathom House. Instead, a large crowd got to see his complete humiliation.

After the victory party, Charlotte and her daughters headed for the Isle of Man. Ironically, they weren't around when Lathom House fell—after all Charlotte's hard work!—in December 1645. This tough-cookie countess outlived the war, and even her husband, who was executed for his part in it. (She did try to get him off the hook, offering to trade: "The Isle of Man for a man—what do you say?") Rich in years, Charlotte survived to bore her neighbors half to death with her tales of the civil war—and her Heroick Countess role in it.

FROM SLAVE TO
SULTANA, WITH WIT

On the streets of Constantinople, this ravishing redhead was called Rossa. Not that **Roxelana** got to *spend* any time on the streets of Constantinople—as a slave of Sultan Suleyman, this exotic import didn't get out much. Bought and sold several times, she'd seen more returns than a salad shooter at K-Mart. After the sultan snapped her up, his PR people got to work, devising a glamorous background for her.

Roxelana had a powerful mind behind her loquacious charm. Her first two years in the harem, she memorized the teachings of the Koran and learned to speak Turkish, Arabic, and Persian. Naturally she learned to sing, dance, sling a veil, and do all that voodoo that slave girls do do so well.

Besides her lessons, Roxelana analyzed the power structure of the harem. Since the sultan's mom ran things, she was the person to suck up to. The newcomer also built a network of female allies by doing favors and telling jokes. Famous for her lilting laugh, she was soon voted "Life of the Harem."

At length, the day came when Suleyman, making the rounds, threw her the white handkerchief. That night Roxelana provided a thrill the sultan had seldom seen: she laid her best stories on him.

(She even made him laugh once or twice.) With this firepower, the other concubines didn't stand a chance. Suleyman started writing love poems to Roxelana, giving her courtside seats at the festivals and beheadings, and so forth.

Forget cooking or sex—humor's the way to a sultan's heart.

177

With her skill at intrigue, it was child's play for Roxelana to bump and grind the Big Four concubines (and their heirs) from the top slots. Before long, the sultan had given Roxelana so many sparkly gifts that she was wealthy. One day she said, "I'd like to give something back to the little people." As he applauded, she added, "But the laws of Islam don't permit slaves to be benefactors. . . . " A significant pause later, Roxelana was freed. After building a hospital or two, she went into Phase Two.

As the sultan prepared to jump her bones one night, she said, "Gosh, now that I'm a freedwoman, this is another religious no can do. To have sex with you, why, I'd have to be . . . married!" Another significant pause. To the mass amazement of Ottoman Turks and Europeans alike, in 1530 wedding bells rang for Roxelana and the sultan—the first harem knot ever tied that wasn't made of real rope.

Now empress (and didn't *that* have a nice sound), the ex-slave luxuriated in her position, producing three sons for job security. Thanks to a huge fire in 1541, much of the original palace burned down. Clutching her Martha Stewart mags, Roxelana began to redecorate— a relaxing task that occupied her until her death in 1558, when she left the world, still laughing.

VERY UPLIFTING
MISTRESS ROLE MODEL

ven in bosom-happy, hang-loose Renaissance times, **Agnes Sorel** stuck out. Really stuck out. Immortalized by a famous painter, posing as the Madonna with child, the mistress and dominatrix of wimpy King Charles VII of France was a breed apart. Her "bustin' out all over" portrait by Jean Fouquet became the mainstay of the new bodice undergarment industry.

Besides exposing two boobs and making another one happy, Agnes enjoyed twenty great years as a royal yenta, matchmaker, and influence peddler at court. The king was OK, but Agnes preferred to pal around with her best friends—who happened to be the king's wife Marie and his mother-in-law Yolande of Anjou.

Declared "official mistress," the first femme in the land of croissants to win that title, Agnes bore the king a passel of daughters and died after childbirth in 1450. You think the king was devastated? You shoulda seen his wife Marie, who instantly moved out. Without Agnes to share the burden, the queen was not about to go it alone with the likes of Charlie.

MRS. GOOD AND PLENTY

cience" might be interesting, but most English folk still relied on good old astrology to answer their questions. Take **Alice Blague** and her chaplain husband Thomas. They became platinum card clients of Simon Forman, the favorite astrologer of everyone, including Good Queen Bess.

Red-haired Alice, with a figure warmly described by her astrologer as "good and comely," had a number of hobbies: dancing, singing, and good cheer. Forman himself got a taste of that good cheer at one point, when the two took a psychic break for a quickie. Free with money as well as her affections, Alice spent an amazing amount of time in taverns, hanging out with prostitutes and local layabouts, and conducting none-too-discreet love affairs. Her stargazer noted in his diary that Alice "did much over-rule her husband," and although "lewd of conversation, she came across 'as holy as a horse.'"

In between one-night stands, Alice became enamored of Dean Wood, a Welch clergyman notorious for "occupying" women from his maid to other men's wives. She stepped up her star sessions to ask, "Would Dean continue 'his faithful love'?" A few months later, she gloomily brought in a list of Dean's lovers, and asked what would become of them. Throwing caution to the winds, Alice even fast-talked husband Thomas into having a horoscope cast on her behalf! "Please ask whether Alice will be enchanted by Dean Wood or not."

The blissfully out-of-it Thomas Blague obliged, meanwhile recasting his own horoscope weekly to see if he'd make bishop, and just what was causing his pesky gout. In 1599, astrologer Simon told Alice that her fiftysomething spouse had gotten gout from too many dates with Rosy Palm. A restive Alice then asked the spirit world just when her husband might be getting on that train to glory. She was a little short of cash: it appears she'd lent money to various male members of the rascally Wood family.

In 1600, when the diaries of Simon Forman came to an abrupt and tantalizing end, the Blagues were still the astrologer's best clients—even though he'd failed to foresee the birth of their daughter Frances, born with a glorious mane of hair that flowed over her entire body. Fortunately for the good and comely Alice Blague, astrologer-client privilege probably kept Thomas from discovering just what on earth she was doing most of the time.

SUED OVER SOFTWARE

o therapists in 1443? No problem; a consummation-starved wife took her woes to court instead. The plaintiff, a **Mrs. Jane Doe,** had plenty to plaint about: she charged that husband John hadn't seen an erection since the early 1400s. A jury of twelve women was assembled in York, England, to see if Mrs. Doe's "can't get no satisfaction" charge was fact or fiction. According to the trial transcript, Mrs. D "exposed her naked breasts . . . held and rubbed the penis and testicles of the said John. And she embraced . . . the said John, and stirred him up in so far as she could to show his virility and potency, admonishing him . . . to prove and render himself a man. . . . The said penis was scarcely three inches long . . . without any increase." Faced with this flabby but undeniably *prima facie* evidence, the women jurors arose, "cursed John for not being better able to serve and please his wife," and left the court. Now annulled for greener pastures, Mrs. Doe had won legal satisfaction at least.

TAKES A VET TO PICK A VET

Born filthy rich in 1657 and the sole heir to daddy's fortune, witty and charming **Catherine Sedley** was a matchmaker's dream. For years, however, she refused to make a match. What she craved was independence of movement—horizontal and vertical.

A skinny girl with an acid tongue, she had the good fortune to live during the anything-goes era of English King Charles II. Soon after becoming maid of honor to the duke's wife, she was doing the duke. When the duke became King James II, Cathy rose to the top as well. Installed as his mistress (although far from the sole one), she had an annual allowance of four thousand pounds, a nice mansion in St. James' Square, and two titles. Even when the next king—who couldn't abide her—came to power, he kept her pension going. (He was afraid not to, it was said.)

At age thirty-eight, Cathy astonished all by deciding to call it quits on the sexual adventures. She'd already turned down marriage nibbles from the likes of the first Sir Winston Churchill. Instead, she chose to marry a Scottish army vet, had two sons, and enjoyed two decades in the wedded state before leaving this Earth at age sixty. Honest as well as sharp-tongued, Cathy often told her boys, "If someone calls you the son of a whore, you must bear it, for you are so. But if they call you bastards, fight until you die—for you are an honest man's sons."

LOBBYIST FOR FLOOZY-FRIENDLY LODGING

pal and playmate of painter Tintoretto and the occasional French king, **Veronica Franco** could turn a phrase as neatly as she could turn a trick. And did both, by turns, from her plush pad in sixteenth-century Venice. A former doctor's wife, Ronnie said Hah! to the conventional traits that made women "desirable": chastity, obedience, and silence. In her well-received poetry, she invited love, admiration, and comparison with the fabled Amazons, which her age saw as the superwomen of history.

Art was admirable, but business was business: Mrs. Franco had no reluctance about appearing in the hookers' Yellow Pages of 1570, a catalog of 215 female names and addresses that also told the world Veronica's age (twenty-nine) and pay-per-view (two ducats). Another source from the era listed her price at four to five crowns per kiss (a sum it would take six months for a servant to earn), and up to fifty crowns for a full-court press.

Veronica wasn't just a me, me, me sort of girl. In her riper years, she became an activist for high-priced courtesans and sexual workers with more modest fees, petitioning the Senate of Venice to help her set up a hospice and hooker refuge. A city jammed with thousands of prostitutes of every category, Venice had a tremendous shortfall of trollop-friendly digs. Along with a decent place to stay, Franco got something going that working women have always needed, ladies of the night no less than the rest: daycare, of course.

I'll throw in the bare boobs, but poetry and ordering off the menu cost extra.

She fired when ready

aura Cereta of Brescia, Italy, got an unusual educational start. Her pop, a military engineer who built fortifications while moonlighting as a physician, took her along on his journeys to distant cities. Although a job site might seem like an unpromising classroom, Laura loved his tutoring in mathematics, Latin, and Greek. Later, she rounded out her curriculum with astrology, classical lit, and moral philosophy.

When puberty hit, Laura didn't get an exemption from the marriage-go-round—but at least she wed an understanding fellow. Each night, after the household had gone to bed, she continued her studies. (That schedule might explain why she didn't get pregnant.)

Eighteen months after marriage, Laura's husband Pietro died of the plague. She was devastated; where the heck would she ever find another male as accommodating?

Now more than ever, Laura turned to her work as therapy. Instead of solo study, however, she now spent her time writing to other scholars, wanting to get into the mainstream of humanism. Most of the humanists who received Cereta's letters either ignored her or fired barbs. What really stung were the snide remarks she got from some female humanists. Livid Laura didn't just brood over her mail. She prepared a salvo of written rebuttals, a form of writing called the "invective." She became the SCUD missile of Italian humanism, hitting male and female targets alike. Rebutting a female rival, she wrote, "I might have forgiven those pathetic men, doomed to rascality, whose patent insanity I lash with unleashed tongue. But I cannot bear babbling and chattering women, glowing with drunkenness and wine, whose impudent words harm not only our sex but even more themselves. . . . Any women who excel they seek out and destroy with the venom of their envy."

Laura's only published work, the first volume of her letters, appeared in 1488—the same year her father died. The loss of her support network of one, coupled with carping critics, threw this young humanist into a crisis. Intellectually, Cereta tossed in the towel. She didn't marry again, or enter a nunnery, or fire off any more invectives (that we know of) in her meager thirty years of life. Her words still have staying power: "The free mind, not afraid to labor, presses on to attain the good."

GLAD TO GIVE "MRS." A MISS

People acted as though she'd dumped a chamber pot on the banquet table when she offhandedly told another woman in King Charles II's court, "Compared to the inconveniences of marriage, its pleasures are so trifling that I don't know how anybody can make up their minds to it." Oldest in the covey of Maids of Honor that surrounded the Duchess of York, the delightfully acid **Miss Hobart** (also spelled Herbert) henceforth got shocked reviews. Courtiers sarcastically called her "Mrs. H." in air quotes. Some abjectly threatened males went further, claiming Hobart was a lesbian. Satirical ballads circulated, labeling her a hermaphrodite. But the most hair-raising story around the water cooler was the tale that the outspoken Hobart had actually gotten a maid pregnant—then fired her. Granted, the folks in Restoration England believed a lot of peculiar things—but that notion certainly took the farthingale. Given the badly skewed ratio of eligible males to females in seventeenth-century England, this maid of honor's ability to be happy sans husband should have gotten an Order of the Garter from the king.

Anti-marriage? Vocally!

BANNED IN BARCELONA

While Europeans of every class and country feared the plague, ran away from it, or tried a variety of useless and repugnant remedies against it, Spanish writer and philosopher **Oliva Sabuco de Nantes Barrera** did something more substantial. When she was twenty-five, she took a running start at an ambitious project with the catchy title of *New Philosophy on the nature of man, unknown to ancient philosophers, which will improve human health and life,* a seven-volume opus that included her best speculations about the causes of plague. Like other medical writers and experts of her day, she was wrong. Instead of an airborne toxin, as Oliva believed, the plague got where it was going via infected fleas on the most common animal in the Renaissance household: *Rattus rattus,* the black rat.

Upon publication in 1587, Oliva got her first break: the Spanish Inquisition denounced her book! Even better, they burned the hardcovers. (Literate risk-takers made a run on the remaining copies—and today, fragments of just two have been found.)

Once this print run is toast,
we'll be back to press in no time!

189

DON'T MESS WITH A PRINTER WITH A BIBLE IN HER HAND

One of only thirty-nine printers in mid-1600s England to receive a patent from the king, **Hester Ogden** had a heck of a time getting out her magnum opus, called *The Sincire and True Translation of the Holy Scripture into the Englishe tounge.* Lack of a spellchecker, you say? More like a copyright dispute. Seems that hard-working Hester wasn't the only printer to get the patent (the privilege of publishing a certain book or edition) for *Sincire and True.* The daughter of a Dr. Fulkes, himself a printer with a king's patent, Hester sought to take over his license, first squeezing some well-fixed friends to lend her start-up cash. But the king had an official printing arm, called His Majesty's Printers, who filed an appeal, saying that Mistress Ogden was infringing on "their" book. Too late: despite their yelps, Hester got the nod to print and sell this particular Bible edition for twenty-one years.

Did Hester herself woman the presses and put ink to paper? We don't know. It's clear, however, from the records left by the Stationers' Company (the English guild of printers) that some girl apprentices and journeywomen did do sweaty, hands-on work as feeders and loaders for England's presses.

Until printers like Hester came along, books were deluxe items, commissioned by the very well-heeled. But by the early 1500s, a copy of the New Testament cost only a day's wages for the average worker—making the printed word a democratic delight. More than any other invention, books spread the ideas—good and bad—of the Renaissance. Between 1500 and 1600, an astonishing 200 million books were printed in Europe by the likes of Hester Ogden.

BEAM ME UP, BILLY!

urious **Margaret Lucas Cavendish** utterly lacked the quality most esteemed by men in her times—female modesty. As a result, this matron with a taste for weird science and weirder fashion ensembles got called a lot of names, most of them unprintable.

Youngest of the large and well-fixed Lucas clan, Maggie was barely eighteen when the English Civil War broke out. She logged on as a lady-in-waiting to Queen Henrietta-Maria, then followed the job—and the queen—into exile in 1644.

In Paris, she met fortyish widower Bill Cavendish, a marquis rich only in bickering children. The two had lots in common. "You're in exile as a royalist sympathizer? Me too!" "You're broke? Me too!" Kismet: the two married, later moving back to England for a legal battle over the Cavendish estate. Bill, who'd majored in sports at Cambridge, had a brother Charles who was a serious geek. Cheered on by Bill, Charles mentored his sister-in-law in science.

Excited by the topic, Margaret turned her new knowledge of scientific theory into a book. Although nonfiction, she called her work *Poems and Fancies,* assuring readers (if any) that it was all fantasy. A self-proclaimed "effeminate Writer," Maggie went on to publish additional books on science, biography, poetry, and plays.

The notoriety was nice—she got great fan mail from famous intellectuals. What Margaret, now the Duchess of Newcastle, really craved, though, was an invite to the Royal Society, *the* exclusive all-boy group of scientists. In 1667, she finally got one.

To dazzle the duchess, Society members weighed air and performed other classy experiments like dipping roast mutton into sulfuric acid, turning it into, quote, pure blood. Later the members made fun of "Mad Madge," dumping on her ideas, her taste in clothes, and above all, her ballsy writing about science—as if a woman, my dear, could know about such matters!

Off base as some of Margaret's ideas may have been, she based them on beliefs held by scientists in her day: a hodgepodge of fact, fallacy, and fantasy, in other words. Maybe that's why she chose to write about science in a fictional format, with women characters getting the juicy parts as scientists and world leaders. (Hmm—that makes Cavendish one of the world's first sci-fi authors, doesn't it?)

But Margaret's greatest contribution was her assertion that the European educational system, rather than the female brain, was feeble. Superlatively self-confident, made more so by an admiring husband and brother-in-law, brash Maggie simply mowed down the simpering conventions of her times. In doing so, she made the female pursuit of science, journalism, and other intellectual endeavors seem desirable—if not respectable.

FAKING IT

An English actress famous for playing Roxelana (the real-life harem beauty who'd become the first Sultana), **Hester Davenport** loved play-acting with a passion. Filthy-rich admirer Lord Oxford had a passion too—and dropped hints about "taking care of her." Despite her actress wages being despicably lower than those of her fellow actors, Hester merely smiled. Oxford threw gifts, favors, insults, and love spells her way; no results. At length he brought up the "m" word: a signed contract of marriage.

Then Oxford did a fair job of play-acting himself, since tying the knot with an actress was still a felony in the 1660s. He put together a bogus ceremony, with musicians subbing as minister and witnesses. (The cake was real, however.) Post-marriage, Oxford awoke Hester with the tender words, "I'll call ya!" Learning that the wedding was a sham, Hester grabbed her fake husband's all-too-real sword and ran him through. A flesh wound, not to worry.

Her anger vented, Hester and Oxford continued as a couple until a child materialized a few years later, whereupon Hester took her paternity grievance to the king. The actress pulled out all stops: besides a large pension, she won the lifetime right to call herself the Countess of Oxford—even after she married (for real this time) some other sniffy aristocrat.

In contrast to Hester's happy ending, the eighty other actresses who trod the boards in the English theater between 1660 and 1689 often got sexually (and monetarily) harassed on the job as well as off. **Rebecca Marshall,** for instance, got a restraining order from the king, no less, against an overenthusiastic fan—who then hired a thug to pelt her with excrement on her way home.

Although theater management had rules against backstage visitors, males in the audience ignored them entirely. Even leading ladies like **Elizabeth Barry** and **Anne Bracegirdle** found themselves dressing (and undressing) in front of uninvited male eyes. Still, what's a bit of bod—the show must go on. Bracegirdle, who gained fame for both tragic and comic roles, kept mum about her private life, which was frustratingly exemplary, according to

Wanna date an actress?
Gimme a sample of your grovel.

theater gossip. Barry, acknowledged as the top dramatic actress of her day, reigned for thirty-three years and even achieved that SAG fantasy: a piece of the action, owning shares in the second company she helped form. Except for a time-out hither and yon with a titled honey, hardheaded Barry stayed single and solo—a state of affairs which earned her character attacks noted for their viciousness. Fortunately, the attacks were but mere words, the raw material Barry worked with every day.

CAREER

Virgins,

SAINTLY
SOULS &

Wa-a-ayward Women

MARRIED TO MUSIC

Who says that homeless or illegitimate girl children couldn't get a break in Renaissance Italy? In Venice they could. From the early 1500s on, four *Ospedali*, or large hospitals with orphanages attached, took in huge numbers of little girls—then trained hundreds of them to be classical musicians, vocalists, soloists, music copyists, composers, and conductors. Sound crazy? Read on.

Lacking last names, the girls got musical handles or took the name of their Ospedali. For example, **Prudenza da Contralto** sang. **Madalena dal Violin** played fiddle. **Zabetta of the Incurabili** was a warbler from the Hospital for the Incurables. Concerts at the Pietà, the most famous of the four orphanages, featured a full orchestra and chorus. In later centuries, musically talented girls who weren't orphans could also join, except at the Pietà, which remained for foundlings only.

All of the glitter folk of Venice attended the Saturday, Sunday, and holiday performances, the ticket revenues going to support the orphanages. One awestruck performance-goer described his night at the Pietà: "They sing like angels, and play violin, flute, oboe, organ, cello, and bassoon, not even stopping at the largest instruments. Some forty girls perform at each concert. There is no more delightful sight than a pretty young nun wearing a white robe and a bouquet of pomegranate flowers in her hair, leading an orchestra with incomparable grace and the proper feeling. The lightness of attack and the purity of tone of their voices is simply divine. . . ."

The girls weren't nuns, however—but they did wear white robes or matching dresses. Their discipline (including fines and bad haircuts for tardiness!) did resemble a convent—except they got much better eats. At the Pietà, training could start as early as three years old for a promising nightingale. After the youngsters became oldsters, they could continue as musicians. Even more staggering, these married-to-music women earned income, invested it, and bequeathed it to whomever they wanted! Wild, huh? If an Ospedali girl chose to marry or join a nunnery, no hard feelings either. She got a dowry and a hearty Brava! from the institution.

Many of these women became virtuosas, famous far beyond Venice. Visitors to the city knew that if you hadn't been to an Ospedali performance, you hadn't "done" Venice. Fans argued over favorites; **Margarita from the Mendicanti** was often compared to Zabetta, who had a violin-like tone in her throat.

The girls were taught by leading music teachers, among them the finest male musicians of the day, who fought over these well-paid jobs. One teacher and musician who spent forty years working at the Ospedali Pietà was none other than Antonio Vivaldi, a former priest whose musical compositions (notably, "The Four Seasons") have again shot to the top in the twentieth century.

House rules: Arrive late for aria
practice, get a bad haircut.

MAKE MINE A
MAIDENHEAD . . . MAYBE

s a girl, **Mariana Alcoforado** never had a yen for a religious calling. But then, she wasn't consulted. Her parents dumped her into a convent in Beja, Portugal, because it was a reputable place to stash a superfluous daughter. At sixteen, she took her vows to become a permanent fixture. A few years later, however, her dad swung by the nunnery to say, "How'd you like to take a spiritual half-time break and come home?"

As it transpired, Mariana's mother had died, leaving another daughter inconveniently lying around, a three-year-old named Peregrina. With dad's help and the nunnery's OK, Mariana set about caring for her sister in a small apartment near the convent.

Then a war involving the French came to little old Beja. Mariana couldn't help checking out the troops in their nice tight uniforms as they paraded by. When her brother introduced her to his regiment officer, a captain named Noel Bouton de Chamilly, she recognized the parade ground specimen she'd been drooling over.

Equally *enchanté*, Captain Noel went after Mariana with ardor. "Hey—no touching—I'm a nun," she said, eluding his caresses. Soon, however, Mariana got addicted to the intense spiritual conversations she had with Captain Noel, but in 1666 he shipped out with his regiment to Andalusia, Spain. By then, Mariana was kicking herself about her "body and soul" policy to the church.

When Chamilly returned to Beja, a by-now incandescent Mariana became his mistress in a Lisbon minute. The carnal revels, while rewarding, weren't quite enough. Mariana longed for a larger commitment. Just then, the war ended, and a scandal-phobic Chamilly bolted back to France, a "Thank you, Lord" on his lips.

Their story would have remained untold had it not been for Mariana's bold action afterward. In the ashes of the affair, she had the nerve to write five letters over the next six months to Captain Noel. After he caddishly read them aloud to his friends, they some-how got into the hands of a Parisian publisher, who came out with them in January 1669. (Mariana would have been about twenty-nine at the time.)

In them, she alchemized her pain and love into literature. In one letter, she says, "Adieu; love me forever; and make me suffer more." Eventually, Alcoforado's letters became the diamonds of Portuguese love poetry; she was called by French novelist Stendhal, "a soul on fire." And the fiery one herself? Purged of rancor and her virginity, she dug out her habit and returned to the nunnery, living to a serene and pious eighty-three.

say two hail marys & call me in the morning

An Italian nun who logged in *molto* hours on her knees in the early 1400s, **Sister Sara of Ferrara** found that, when it came to miracles, she got the best results by praying local. One day, she caught wind of an ugly situation: The head honcho of Ferrara was arranging a duel between two Spanish knights, one of whom was sure the other had killed his slave. Aghast (at the duel, unfortunately, not at the notion of slavery), Sister Sara set to work. A couple of marathon genuflection sessions later, one of the combatants withdrew his challenge and the duel was canceled. Certain that her time in a spiritual chat room had done the trick, Sister Sara bounced off to commission a painting of her feat.

The finished work, done in 1432, is still around. It portrays two knights exchanging a kiss (of peace, not sudden passion). No shrinking violet, the good sisiter had herself portrayed front-and-center in the picture ("Make sure you get my good side!") ostentatiously praying at the feet of Saint Francis of Assisi.

Sara wasn't alone in leaning on saintly powers. However, soon it didn't seem good enough to merely pray—people felt they needed to guarantee results by paying a fee called an indulgence. That led, in part, to an explosion of indulgence sales—and further on, a disgusted reaction to it, called Protestantism.

ḣabitual ḣumor

An obscure nun from an obscure corner of Portugal, **Violante do Céu** was born to the Montesino family around the beginning of the seventeenth century and lived nearly one hundred years. This centenarian could rock: besides being a poet and a playwright, she was a mean musician. But her most fabulous accomplishment (at least from our point of view) may be her curiously twentieth-century sense of humor. For instance, take the wonderfully surreal title that she gave one of her poems in a book called *Rimas Varias* that she created at age forty-four. Given the length and the intricacy of the title, some might even praise it as a poem unto itself: "Voice of a Dissipated Woman Inside a Tomb, Talking to Another Woman Who Presumed to Enter Church with the Purpose of Being Seen and Praised by Everyone, Who Sat Down Near a Sepulchre Containing This Epitaph, Which Curiously Reads."

The it girl

inon de Lenclos could have made coffee nervous, the way she kept at it nonstop. "It" being the high-end mistress business, that is. Beginning at sixteen, this French tickler fulfilled the needs of a duke, a count, a couple of marquis, two military marshals, and an abbot or two in her seventy-year career. Luckily, she was a woman who loved her work. As Ninon said more than once, "If anyone had proposed a life of chastity to me, I should have hanged myself."

Born Anne Lenclos, she quickly grew into a brilliant beauty, famed for wit and style. Providing TLC for the passing parade of eminent men in her life took up much of her time. There was an occasional holiday for a discreet baby or two, but Ninon wasn't up to childrearing. She had them raised by others, unaware of her.

As the years passed, Ninon de Lenclos developed such a reputation for good taste that she became almost respectable. As a sideline, she began to give Miss Manners—like classes to kids from the best families, whose *mamans* paid big bucks for lessons in *savoir faire.* Lenclos knew she'd reached the pinnacle of fame when she became the subject of a roman à clef novel written by another woman—a best-seller in ten volumes, no less.

A lifelong religious skeptic, Ninon eventually got into hot water for mouthing off. Anne, the stiff-lipped queen mother of France,

took offense at her iconoclastic views (to say nothing of her décol-
letage), and in 1659, she came down cruelly hard. Instead of sending
her to a jail, the queen banished poor Ninon to a convent.

To pass the weary hours sans male company or even a decent
croissant, Mademoiselle Lenclos sat down and wrote her own book,
called *The Vengeance of a Coquette,* and concealed it in her underwear until
she could find a publisher. Among its memorable lines: "We should
take care to lay in a stock of provisions, but not of pleasures: these
should be gathered day by day."

About that time, a by-product of Ninon's past pleasures entered
the picture. Now in her Mae West period, Ninon really went for hot
young suitors. Unbeknownst to either party, her latest flame was one
of her sons. When he learned the appalling news, the boy committed
suicide. This heartrending event put a real damper on her career mistress game. Ninon de Lenclos turned to milder fare—a Paris salon,
where she hosted an glittering group of playwrights, diplomats, military men, eggheads, and writers, including French philosopher
Voltaire (she became so fond of him that she left Voltaire a legacy in
her will to buy books).

At the end of her long and busy life, Ninon regretted almost
nothing—except the aging process. Her rueful one-liner is still making the rounds, especially in plastic surgeons' offices: "Old age is
woman's hell."

a polish heaven on earth

She might not have known her crustaceans (her coat of arms boasts a critter identified as a crab—we'd call it a lobster) but **Jadwige Gnoinskiej** sure knew how to found a utopian community. Polish-born and an ardent believer in Arianism (a 1500s fad in Protestantism), Jadwige married a nobleman who was a Calvinist. Despite his taste in blue jeans, Jadwige won him over to her sect—then made him cough up enough cash to found Rakow, her new Polish heaven on Earth.

Jadwige's own group called themselves the Polish Brethren; it included sisters, too, whose rights were zealously respected. It didn't take long to get Rakow on the map, despite the confusion of its name with the Polish capitol of Krakow. Settlers to the new utopia received generous chunks of land for a house, garden, and meadows for cattle, and could will them to future generations. With its small city flowing around a lake, surrounded by thick woods, sandy but fertile soil, sunny meadows, and a temperate climate—what could be more idyllic? The Brethren soon had settlers pouring into their new Zion, digging wells and building houses (some of the dwellings are still standing today).

Jadwige and the Rakovians had high ideals. Sworn pacifists, they wore swords made of wood. This proved cumbersome, however. Later

Rakovians would serve only as noncombatants in Poland's incessant wars. There were no official mouthpieces or ministers in the group—everyone had a say. While egalitarian, that also got to be a headache, when all the mouthpieces talked at once.

Women could and did preach, an act of daring that got various mainstream Christian queens of Europe into an uproar. They also had no fear of other preachers. On several occasions, the raucous Rakovian women shouted down a clergyman they didn't take to.

The most delightful aspect of the Brethren was their close-to-utopian community of equals. Besides calling each other "brother" and "sister" (except the slaves, of course), Jadwige's pioneers gave equal weight to everyone's words, from a peasant woman to a middle-class artisan.

For over a century, Rakow and the Polish Brethren thrived, occasionally laughed at for their nondesigner clothing and the spectacle of their female preachers, but tolerated by the larger community of Poland. In 1658, however, the Arian sect and the entire band of Rakovians were banished. The legacy of Jadwige, Our Lady of the Crab, had run its course.

Well, I think that "Jadwige's Utopia"
has a nicer ring.

207

MARTYR MAGNET

hey already had pay-per-view in sixteenth-century Europe; you viewed a saintly relic, then paid a fee or indulgence. Each relic, from the tooth of Saint Jerome to a straw from Jesus' crib, had a precise value that would reduce your time in purgatory. For instance, if you paid to see the collection at Wittenberg, Germany, on Nov. 1 (when they ran an All Saints' Special), you could cut your purgatory stay by 1,902,202 years and 270 days.

Wibrandis Rosenblatt may not have seen the collection—she probably couldn't fit it into her schedule. But if anyone deserved to whiz through purgatory and don heavenly robes, it was her.

She came from a well-fixed Swiss family. There was no pressing need for her to marry and care for one husband, much less four (plus untold kids, stepkids, and family members). But she did. Between 1520 and 1564, she took on four church reformers (all of 'em poor, perennially in trouble with the authorities, often sent into exile, prone to get plague). After theologian Martin Bucer, number four, bit the dust, Wibrandis calmly panhandled her fellow exiles in England to get her and her surviving kids back to Basle. Is there a national monument somewhere to Wibrandis, the supreme coper? If not, shouldn't there be?

"UNYOKED IS BEST!"

 sister in a religious order in Holland, **Anna Bijns** ran her own school and taught during the mid-1500s. Remembered chiefly as a writer, at times Bijns shocked the bejesus out of her audiences. Through her plays and poems, she attacked Lutheranism and the social ills she thought it brought. One of her surviving works was *Marika of Nijmeghen,* an early version of the Faust legend. In it, a female protagonist sells her soul to the devil in return for instruction in the liberal arts (in Anna's day a strange assortment of rhetoric, music, logic, grammar, geometry, arithmetic, and alchemy). You might call the dialogue "wooden"—especially the devil's lines, which invariably begin, "Well, my pretty, you can trust me." Feminist Anna had fresh things to say about female independence, however. She advocated taking a pass on marriage, "even if he's rich and noble," calling the single gal a "lord and mistress, none ever lived better." Did these remarks inflame? I'd say so: For publishing Bijns' first collection of writings, her printer actually got executed!

A Faust-talking woman is the devil's work.

ORGY OVERLOAD? MORE
LIKE MARITAL BURNOUT

Where would the Renaissance be without **Lucrezia Borgia,** the name that stands for lascivious skullduggery? But was Lucrezia really the brother-embracing, poison-lacing princess she was rumored to be? As they say in Italy, "Even if it's not true, it's a good invention."

Born in 1480 to the longest-running affair on record in Rome, Lucrezia was one of the out-of-wedlocks from Rodrigo Borgia (soon to be Pope Alexander) and mistress **Rosa Vanozza.** At twelve, the preteen Goldilocks began her grownup duties, that is, cementing political alliances by marrying. Her first was Giovanni Sforza, who leapt at the chance to become the pope's son-in-law. Held at the Vatican, the June wedding featured 150 maids of honor (and/or dishonor, some of them being the pope's concubines).

This wedding was so much fun that in July 1498, Lucrezia wanted to wed again, only to be told, "You're still Mrs. Sforza." But a quiet visit from Borgia henchmen to her husband, with a hint about what the pope could do to a Sforza's chances of reaching heaven, to say nothing of old age, did the trick. A commission on virginity took mere seconds to find Lucrezia ready to roll: "Your husband was impotent? You're still a virgin? Sounds good to us—will that be cash or charge?"

By this time, the buzz around Rome was "incest"—did hotpants Lucrezia have a thing for her brother and/or her papal daddy? Well, the Borgias did like keeping it all in the family—but the "it" was probably power, not intercourse.

Nevertheless, in 1500, Lucrezia's second mate suffered a series of misfortunes: attacked by "bandits," he escaped, only to succumb to a Borgia specialty, some very bad home cooking.

Soon a happy trio of singles—Lucrezia, her father, and her brother Cesare (now official "helper" to the pope)—gave Rome new depravities to discuss. For instance, the papal orgy contests. With Lucrezia as a referee, fifty nude hookers crawled about the floor, while fifty palace servants did their best to couple with as many as possible. Prizes of silk and jewelry went to those who'd linked limbs with the greatest number.

It wasn't long before Lucrezia hit the marriage market again; somewhat nervously, Alfonso d'Este, the duke of Ferrara, took the bait. And surprise! He lived. Even greater surprise: he gave the gift that kept on giving to the golden girl of the Borgias: "the burning disease," an affliction sweeping Europe. After her eleventh pregnancy (four survived childhood), Lucrezia died at thirty-nine of its complications. A few years later, the burning malady got a name that stuck, taken from a character's name in a popular poem, believe it or not: they called it "syphilis."

whole lotta shaking

lthough **Margaret Fell** and company called themselves the Society of Friends, they quickly got the Quaker label for their go-to-meeting style, described in an indignant 1655 pamphlet as "Shriekings, shakings, quakings, roarings, yellings, howlings, tremblings in the bowels, and risings in the bellies."

Margaret's bowel-trembling came in midlife. A silver-spoon child, at sixteen she married more money (a judge to boot) and had seven brilliant daughters and a son. In her thirties, she came down with a case of spiritual acid indigestion. Then she heard Quaker leader George Fox speak, and an inner light came on. Stunned by her insta-conversion, her husband refused to shriek, quake, or join—but didn't fight her choice in the matter.

In six years, Margaret was both a widow and a big wheel in the Friends. Nicknamed the "nursing mother of Quakerism," she kept the finances going, plagued the king and queen with unsolicited books and letters, and filled in whenever Fox and others were in prison or abroad (a weekly occurrence, by the sound of it). At her Swarthmoor Hall, she built a tradition of philanthropy that became a hallmark of the Society.

In 1664, the widow Fell was charged with "illegal meetings."
After refusing to take a court oath, and being threatened with a life
sentence and seizure of her property, she calmly said, "If the king's
pleasure is to take my estate, on account of my conscience, and not
for any evil or wrong done, let him do as he pleaseth."

He pleaseth, and she was promptly locked into leaky Lancaster
Castle, where George Fox was already serving time (again). Instead of
working on her bench-pressing, Mrs. Fell sat down and wrote the

I want to shimmy like my sister Margaret.

first of sixteen books and pamphlets. *Women's Speaking* was published in 1666; due to leg irons, Fell was unable to do an author tour, and remained behind bars until 1668.

At fifty-five, she and Fox married, delighting everyone except *his* daughter and *her* son—who teamed up for a vendetta against the newlyweds. In 1670, the kids managed to get Margaret returned to jail! Thanks to lobbying from Quaker preacher **Elizabeth Hooton,** Margaret was made an Overseer at Fleet prison, and got to give perks (like regular meals) to inmates. (Strange as it sounds to modern ears, in Ren times many jailers were former inmates.)

By now, the Quaker movement had grown huge. Antiwar and pro-simplicity, the Society of Friends also empowered women; over two hundred became preachers in the 1600s.

Margaret lived over eighty years, arguing to the last that the voice women had gained among the Friends was proof of a new millennium and "the True Church." (Close, but no cigar; Quaker fempower nosedived in later centuries. So did the caliber of membership. In the twentieth century, it included Richard Nixon.)

ANGEL WITH AN ACID TONGUE

Arcangela Tarabotti taught herself to read and write, then penned six books in her lifetime. Two weren't published until this nun was almost to the pearly gates. Can't think why. Who could object to a clamorous indictment of the dowry system entitled *The Convent as Hell?* Her critique of the way convents were run, called *Deceitful Simplicity,* was similarly demure. A reluctant member of her religious community, Arcangela didn't have a true spiritual calling—yet never left the convent of Sant'Anna in Castello, Venice. Why? Perhaps because no better place to think and write existed for a single woman of modest resources in the 1600s. Pro-choice about women's life choices (or rather, lack of them) Arcangela did like one thing: living in a community of women.

Talk about hell on earth—you try grocery shopping for a bunch of nuns!

215

NORDIC TREKKER

ver wonder why depictions of the Virgin Mary are often so Nordic? Courtesy of saintly **Birgitta of Sweden,** that's why. Her highly popular, widely read visions of Mary and the nativity scene eventually became the model for much of Renaissance art, from the Virgin Mary's long golden hair to the choir of angels singing.

The noble daughter of a provincial governor, married at fourteen to another governor, Brigitta logged years as a housewife, baking cookies and raising eight kids, until the Queen of Sweden asked her, "Wanna be a lady-in-waiting?" High-energy Birgitta found the courtly nine-to-five a coffee klatch. To relieve the tedium, she got into religious visions, similar to the ones she'd experienced at age seven.

Right off the bat, she had a knockout rapture about the dubious doings of Sweden's King Magnus. "Better shape up," she told the sheepish monarch. After Brigitta's husband died in 1344, the king even gave her start-up change (hush money, perhaps?) for a new order of nuns and monks. The saintly Swede whizzed around, twisting arms and twitting popes, founding hospices and setting up convents around England and Scandinavia. Canny Birgitta made her convents financially independent by requiring sixty "charter member" nuns to kick in enough land and assets to keep them for life.

Later, Birgitta's fourth daughter, Catherine, joined in the fun of start-ups and pilgrimages—once she'd convinced her new husband that they'd *both* be better off if she stayed a virgin. Not all of Birgitta's kids were holier than her. During Birgitta's Golden Years tour of the Holy Land, she was seriously embarrassed by her married son, who started doing the nasty in Jerusalem with a certain shameless royal hussy. Birgitta kicked herself for not getting trip insurance—the whole thing was a nightmare, from her son's transgressions to a near-shipwreck on the return to Rome.

In perpetual motion until she was in her seventies, this spiritual Swede kept working on her Birgittine franchise until it numbered eighty convents. (Twelve are still active today.) She lobbied for a single language for Scandinavia; when that flopped, she made sure that her 700-plus visions were written down, in Swedish, Norwegian, and Latin.

A warm woman with a laugh like honey, Birgitta became famous for her down-to-earth sayings as well as her visions. She liked her tipple, too. As she once said, "Wine is wholesome, gives health to the sick, joy to the sorrowful, courage and bravery to those who are well."

100-WATT MIRACLE WORKER

"She was small, fair, winsome, and charming, so delicate as to frighten her doctor, for frequently she fainted. . . . Her eyes were a trifle too merry for a saint. . . . She dressed elegantly to show that piety does not consist of a habit."

This adoring description of **Francisca Hernández,** an *alumbrado* or "illuminated one," a member of a mystic sect from Salamanca, Spain, came from one of her miraculous "cures," a monk named Frankie Ortíz. For years, he'd suffered from a trying disorder—trying for a monk, that is. Nicknamed "Wet Dream" Ortíz, his erotic activity not only kept the other monks awake and dirtied an inordinate amount of sheets, but tormented him spiritually. Then he caught wind of Francisca, who had a growing rep in monkish circles as a miracle worker when it came to eliminating those pesky desires of the flesh.

Sure enough, Francisca fixed Frankie and all was serene for a while. About 1525, though, the young expert at lustful liposuction was arrested and imprisoned by the Spanish Inquisition. Frankie protested and was also dungeoned for his pains. For four years, the two were interrogated and tortured. The authorities tried to make Francisca out to be a loose woman. With the help of a branding iron, they got one individual to admit he'd "bundled" her (an all-night rubfest, without actual sex) and "she'd liked it." However, a physical exam showed Hernández was still a virgin.

Although the illuminated ones were frowned on for public preaching, Francisca had many celebrity endorsements. She'd gotten praise from Emperor Charles V's personal priest, and even the Inquisitor General, who later made pope.

But other church authorities still refused to help, saying, "Well, we'd believe her claims—if only she were a nun. If only she weren't illiterate." Her true-blue friend Frankie rebutted by saying that she could interpret Scriptures with more profundity than the most learned doctors. Inquisition officials finally got Ortíz to admit that he'd kissed the ground Francisca walked on; he maintained, however, that he'd stuck to dirt—his lips had never touched any of her body parts.

In an almost unprecedented denouement for that time and place, both were eventually released, alive and unmaimed, by the Spanish Inquisition. Frankie got sent to another monastery. Francisca Hernández, worn but still winsome, got probation.

ph.d. for an underutilized do-gooder

Who says Italian men can't be sensitive? In the mid-1600s, noblewoman **Elena Piscopia** stayed single *and* pursued a life of the mind—encouraged in this feminist folly by her own father!

At nineteen, Elena joined a convent, living at home but wearing a nun's habit under her street clothes. (That must have been murder during Venice's muggy summers.) When nearly thirty, she began a lightweight course load at the U. of Padua: science, theology, math, philosophy, Latin, Greek, Hebrew, Arabic, and Chaldaic. In 1678, Piscopia obtained the first Doctor of Philosophy degree ever awarded to a woman. The university was so swamped with requests for seats to this event that the ceremony had to be moved to a bigger venue at the cathedral. By this time, Elena's reputation was such that scholars from Rome to Siena sat at her feet. She didn't care about any stinking fans—what she wanted was a doctorate in Theology. The school used the "What good will it do you?" premise to deny her—odd, since the same might be said about many fields of study, to say nothing of many scholars.

A disgruntled Piscopia said, "Might as well do a magnum opus on philosophy," and went on to publish a three-volume work, plus doing a little lecturing on topics from math to astronomy.

Thwarted by the establishment, Elena invented her own spiritual ministry by caring for the poor. Perhaps it was in the decaying quarters of Venice that she got tuberculosis. At the news of her demise, the city echoed with the cry, "The saint is dead!" Venice's sadly underutilized genius was mourned by all, which must have been a *wonderful* consolation to Elena and family.

She hardly weighs a thing—must have eaten at the university cafeteria.

BAREFOOT & ECSTATIC

Fasting, flagellation, licking lepers' wounds—all of 'em pretty passé on the piety circuit by the 1550s, when **Teresa of Ávila** was in her prime. Instead, the Spanish nun of Ávila brought a completely new move to the arena—the spiritual equivalent of the triple sow cow. In her trances, she achieved ecstatic "transverberation," defined as a golden lance from God repeatedly piercing her heart. (Doubters may want to view what's described as Teresa's wound-riddled heart, still preserved under glass at her Ávila convent.)

Showing her spiritual colors early, Teresa grew up on the high arid plateaus of Castile, reading trashy romances and daydreaming about being a hermit. At seven, she ran away from home, hoping to reach the Holy Land and become a martyr by getting her head sliced off by the heathens. After her escape fizzled, she became a typical teen: fond of perfume, fancy clothes, and boys. Given that the boy she was most taken with was her cousin, her dad put the kibosh on that relationship by sending her to the local convent for an education.

For years, she lived as a nun at several convents—some of them lax and luxurious. When Teresa's fortieth birthday rolled around, she started getting awful visions of hell that impelled her into action. Besides working on her own soul, and levitating now and then, she reformed the Carmelite order, starting up seventeen new convents. Members had to eat vegetarian, live on alms, and (very important) keep Teresa from going into a trance while cooking dinner.

Some of the sisters liked Teresa's honest austerity more than others; they became the Barefoot Carmelites. The more luxury-loving women with bunion problems stuck to being the Shod Carmelites. Predictably, the Catholic Church opposed her work.

Teresa also wrote three books, including *The Interior Castle,* a work of such excellence that it influenced her friend and fellow Spaniard John of the Cross—and eventually won her the title of Doctor of the Church from the twentieth century's Pope Paul VI.

When this merry, sensible woman died of ill health in 1582, those around her recalled the words that Teresa had written twenty years earlier: "To those who love God in truth and have put aside the things of this world, death must come very gently." And so it did.

It's transverberation time; smite me with that heavenly sword!

ḋARḋCORE CALVIN FAN

It's not often that women *wish* for facial hair. But **Renée of France** did: "If I had a beard I woulda been the King of France!" She was in a huff because she'd been passed over in favor of some shirt-tale male cousin. Once again the Salic law of succession, derived from an incredibly passé fifth-century code, kept a good woman from gaining the throne. Sure, Renée could have tried male hormones, or waited until menopause to see if that hoped-for five o'clock shadow would kick in.

Instead, she got fobbed off on Hercule d'Este, the duke of Ferrara. By now, Renée was sick of the marriage game anyway: she'd been engaged to more kings than she could count—Charles V, Henry VIII, yadda yadda.

To keep busy, the new duchess worked hard to develop the sexiest court circle in Europe, roping in poets, artists, philosophers, and any other free agents with pretensions to high culture. Some of her most glittering grabs were women, including Olimpia Morata, the hot young humanist to watch in the sixteenth century.

A glutton for punishment, Renée turned to childbearing and a new religion, Calvinism, for solace. (She may have been sucked in by the founder's supposed views on the equality of men and women, which later vanished in a cloud of "I was misquoted.")

Although she did a great job of educating her daughter Anne, Renée got a lot of static about following the teachings of Calvin, a forerunner of the Puritan movement. A plain old Catholic himself, the duke got more and more irate. Finally Hercule pulled a strong-arm move, ripping the kids out of Renée's care and banishing her from court until she agreed to give up on that Puritanical nonsense.

Now sullen as all get out, Renée fumed in exile until the duke finally died in 1559. Then she gathered up her inheritance marbles and headed for France to set up an even more glittering court. In a "So hah!" to Hercule the heavy, she made Chez Renée a clearinghouse for Calvinist propaganda.

SPINSTA RAP—
IT'S RAPTURE

chool dropout? "Yes, sirree!" said **Anna Trapnel.** The clever daughter of an English shipwright, she was an untutored yet eloquent prophet of a mid-1600s millennium cult called the Fifth Monarchists. For a time, the group backed commoner Oliver Cromwell over royal rule. That ended when Anna and the Fifths saw that Cromwell was not going to set up a kingdom of heaven on Earth using *their* ground rules. After Cromwell was installed as England's leader anyway, Anna had the habit of falling into raptures outside his council's chambers, logging marathon performances in an ecstatic state. (Her record? Twelve garrulous days.) Eventually she spent two rat-happy months in Bridewell prison. The worst part was being locked up with harlots and thieves—an association that made the fiercely respectable Miss Trapnel swoon—but not in rapture. Despite this treatment, Anna refused to stop prophesying. As late as 1658, her verses were being documented by a reporter; only after Cromwell died that year did Trapnel's trances cease.

SPIRIT IN THE DARK

Being a visionary was burden enough—but the homework really killed you. A teenager from Florence, **Caterina de'Pazzi** left her noble family in 1574 and entered the Carmelite convent of Santa Maria degli Angeli. Now known as Sister Maria Maddalena, she would sit, lost in ecstatic visions, and sew or paint, her eyes fixed unseeing on the heavens. The nuns of her convent got to wondering: Do you think she needs light to do her work? Wouldn't it be, like, really miraculous if she did it . . . say, blindfolded? In a flash, they'd bandaged Sister Maria's eyes and put her in a pitch-dark room for good measure. Sure enough, Caterina continued to paint, using a higher power, or possibly sonar. Her confessor, Father Puccini, wrote: "With her eyes bandaged, she continued the painting she had in hand, with her usual mastery and perfection. And so in trances she carried out much work and many holy pictures which have been preserved as miraculous." Although Sister Maria did other things—such as work her way up the nunnery corporate ladder to become sacristan, and later, vice-prioress, she's most remembered for her after-dark paintings. Eight of her works still exist at a convent named for her near Trespiano, Italy. Modern critics tend to sniff at the poor materials and the unoriginality of the images—but I'll wager that few of them have made it to sainthood, as Caterina did in 1669.

X-RATED VISIONARY

From a hick town near Toledo, Spain, raised by her father, and later an aunt and uncle, **Juana de la Cruz** had her eye on a life of holiness from the start, warming up with a series of fits and visions. Her relatives didn't buy it. "You're getting married," they said. Before any rice got flung, Juana flew the coop, running away from home in some manly garments left around the house. The nunnery she ran to, in the hamlet of Cubas, wasn't all that thrilled to welcome a cross-dressing teen with zero cash for a dowry. Juana, however, got her relatives to cough up so she could join.

By 1509, thanks to the entrancing sermons she gave while trancing, she'd been elected abbess. She started getting fan mail—some of it weird stuff, like the offer from a randy Franciscan, who wanted Juana to be the mom of a new Messiah that the two of them would procreate. Juana quickly filed a delusional Messiah restraining order, and that guy was history.

Her next battle wasn't so easy. Stoked by jealous officials, the church tried to annex her nunnery; Mother Juana had to spend big bucks to get a papal bull (read: bribe) in their favor. Things finally quieted down enough so that Juana could spend the next thirteen years having mystical raptures. During her six-hour trances, she gave long allegorical sermons.

One of her spiritual companions took on the onerous chore of writing down a year's worth of Juana's ecstatic musings. The results made strange reading, revolving around the mostly nude antics and

dance moves of the Virgin Mary, depicted as a girl child with grownup Barbie breasts. Despite her spirituality, today's historians can't help but wonder about what abuse Juana may have seen in her early life—or what loco weed she might have been growing in the convent garden.

Parental consent needed to view these visions.

229

SHE PUT THE "HER"
IN LUTHERAN

"'m distressed that our princes take the Word of God no more seriously than a cow does a game of chess." That acerbic comment, and many more like it, came from the often-quoted mouth of **Argula von Grumbach,** a German intellectual and noblewoman of Bavaria. Noted for being pro-Lutheran, her reputation as a clear-thinking writer has largely vanished (or worse yet, been confused with a trendy variety of lettuce found in yuppie salads). In her day, though, Argula's activism was noticed—and punished.

In 1523, incensed over the treatment of a young male teacher with Lutheran leanings at the University of Ingolstadt, she fired off letters to the university, Martin Luther, ruler Frederick the Wise of Saxony, the city council, and her local duke of Bavaria to protest. Did she get any thank-you-for-sharing notes, or even a lousy sound bite on the Bavarian PBS station? She did not.

What she did get was instant underground notoriety stemming from the unauthorized publication of her letters—followed by a merrily anonymous satire about Argula, hinting that she must be (1) sexually frustrated despite her marriage and thus (2) hot for the young teacher whom she defended. In spite of her husband's grumbling, Argula once again took pen in hand and answered the scurrilous poem with a serious yet scathing set of her own verses.

230

Rather than attack the articulate Mrs. Grumbach herself, authorities conveyed displeasure through her husband. "Get in there and control your wife!" he was told. To rub it in, he lost out on a sure-thing plum position—and now he had a valid reason to gripe.

For her part, Argula just kept right on being a committed Lutheran, not seeing anything extraordinary or courageous in her actions. As she once said in a letter to the city council: "If I die, a hundred women will write to you, for there are many who are more learned and adept than I am." Hooray for von Grumbach, upon whose unflinching beliefs the Lutheran religion was built. And just how often did Argula (or any women, for that matter) get credit where credit was due from Martin Luther himself? Anybody know the German word for "zip"?

BIG BRAINS MAKE
STRANGE BEDFELLOWS

Lucky **Isotta** and **Ginevra Nogarola**—not only did these sisters share a thirst for knowledge, they came from a Veronese family that honored female learning by footing the bill! Their own mom paid for their education. A widow, she didn't have to answer to any stinking male relatives about the cost of their pricey tutor, either.

Raved about by their teens, the Nogarola sisters chose to be humanists—the curriculum for any self-respecting scholar of fifteenth-century Italy. In 1437, however, Isotta found herself between a book and a hard place. Her fan mail had slowed; she was assaulted verbally by a growing number of males who wanted to keep her out of their intellectual boys-only club and ridiculed by other learned women in Veronese society. To top it off, her older sister Ginevra bailed on her by getting married.

Then things got really ugly: an anonymous letter circulated, accusing her of promiscuity *and* incest with her brother! (A natural conclusion, according to some: after all, "everybody knew" that big-brained women craved unnatural lust.)

No wonder Isotta pledged herself to permanent virginity and dove for cover into the religious life. In her convent room, she prayed, studied, and corresponded with the other thinkers who were still talking to her. Despite the curtain of privacy Isotta had drawn between herself and the world, a dashing former governor named Ludovico Foscarini got a crush on her. Of course, he concealed it with a lot of rhetoric about her vows of sanctity and his own marital woes. Now and then, however, he managed to penetrate her cell for a visit, recalling them in his journal with unpious breathlessness.

Nogarola must have given off powerful pheromones; at thirty-five, she got a marriage proposal from another admirer. Foscarini immediately chided her with Freudian fervor, saying, "It wasn't proper that she should even think about that libidinous cohabitation called 'marriage.'"

Cohabit, she didn't. Engage in full frontal debate over sexual identity, she did. Isotta even called Foscarini's bluff at one point, suggesting that he give up his worldly life and join her by taking religious orders. (He scuttled away from that one in record time!) Isotta's surviving dialogue with Foscarini over these matters may be the most interesting document she ever wrote.

Isotta Nogarola died in holy solitude at forty-eight. Even in her supposedly "enlightened" times, she found that a big-brained gal needed a hard hat to survive the rage that female achievements sometimes aroused.

What does it take to get some quality time alone in this convent??

THE

Mrs.,
Misses
&
Near Misses

OF

KING HENRY VIII

amous as a philanthropist, college founder, patron of religious houses, and ruler, **Margaret Beaufort** was one of *the* Plantagenets of Tudor England—and the carrot-topped granny of Henry VIII.

She went into labor with Henry VII about the time her husband, Edmund Tudor, lay imprisoned and dying, as the English Civil War between the houses of York and Lancaster raged. On January 28, 1457, the sweaty but proud fourteen-year-old mother wrote: "This day of Saint Agnes, I did bring into this world my good and gracious prince."

Margaret's next husband, Stafford, was a prince, too—educating her boy and making Mom the wealthy wife of a knight. He didn't last, either, and after four marriages and funerals, Margaret took a "been there, done that" attitude, concentrating instead on her son as the first Tudor king.

In 1485, she pulled it off. On the q.t., she'd gotten rebellious nobles to support her son's bid, and bought chunks of English lands for him. Post-coronation, a grateful son gave Margaret her own small queendom. Even better, he and Parliament let her run it the way she wanted, just as any owner with a codpiece would do.

One of the world's most demanding readers, patron Margaret was leaning over the shoulder of printer William Caxton when the first book published in English came off the press in 1476. She also picked up the tab for the publication of religious works, and put out serious money to endow university chairs at Oxford and Cambridge.

True, the prison system didn't have the glamour of a first edition unveiling or a university opening, but Margaret directed her philanthropy there, too. She even allowed photo ops, being pictured in paintings on her visits to lockup, chatting with prisoners through the bars, while a servant held her fur-trimmed train off the unspeakably filthy floors.

Margaret kept active until her death in 1509; for two years prior, she'd been High Commissioner for the Council of the North, acting as justice of the peace and rendering judgments still on record. The year she died, a grandson with her energy and reddish-gold hair began his reign as King Henry VIII. Later, the crown of England would be placed on the strawberry blonde hair of Elizabeth I, the great-granddaughter of the indomitable Beaufort—whose name means "beautiful and strong."

ADAMANT COMES
IN SMALL PACKAGES

nyone want a slightly used infanta? was the word around the English court in 1502, when rosy-cheeked **Catherine of Aragon** saw her fifteen-year-old husband, Prince Arthur, die (probably of the sweating sickness) just four months after marriage. Before expiring, the frail and boyish groom was said to have boasted, "I've been in Spain all night."

In no-maiden's land as far as virginity status, and still at sea learning English 101, the petite and sweet-natured teen widow was then engaged to Art's brother, Henry. After seven years of financial hardship (thanks to a dowry tug-of-war between her cheap father-in-law and her stingy dad) Catherine wed the man who was now King Henry VIII of England, in 1509.

Oh boy, Catherine anticipated, smooth sailing—and in the beginning, love (at least on her side) did blossom. In his buffed-out, blue-eyed, energetic prime, Henry in turn bragged about his wedding night with Catherine, saying he'd found her "still a maid." (It seems clear that Arthur's "travels to Spain" were just virtual ones.)

For a political liaison, Catherine and Henry grew remarkably close. But the years rolled by, marked by miscarriages. Then came the most terrifying words a postpartum queen could hear: "It's a girl!" The birth and survival of baby Mary in 1516 began the decline of

Henry's interest in this intelligent and educated woman.

What a waste of womanpower. Trained to rule, Catherine had been given a brilliant education, thanks to her mother, Queen **Isabel la Católica**, who steeped herself in Latin, French, and philosophy with her daughters. Catherine had studied with the greats, including Spain's most famous female savants—**Beatriz Galindo** and **Francisca de Lebrija.**

During her twenty-two years as Queen of England, Catherine promoted humanism and was a loyal patron of Dutch humanist Erasmus. A pioneer for women's education, the queen commissioned the first handbooks ever written on the subject for her daughter Mary.

She might have been short and sweet, but Catherine's demeanor concealed sheer guts. When Henry fell for Anne Boleyn in 1526 and wanted to shed his first queen pronto, Catherine stood up to him, the pope, Cardinal Wolsey, and other political powers for eight years. She never did grant the guy a divorce. Never. The irascible king then invented his own no-fault dissolution and a new state religion with himself as its head. To her dismay, Catherine became the catalyst that brought the Church of England into being.

Their mutual failure to make a living male heir also led to Henry's deplorable marriage-go-round of six wives. Too bad the king didn't just go with the flow and let his daughters Mary and Elizabeth rule. Isn't it odd that *that* is what happened anyhow?

Living in a
Prophesy-free Zone

Being vocal about the future—especially if you're calling the clairvoyancy shots on an aggressively nutty king bent on shedding a wife—could be inflammatory, as **Elizabeth Barton,** a.k.a. **the Holy Maid of Kent,** found out. After an illness in the 1520s, this wild-eyed young epileptic with a religious streak started going into noisy trances. Most of her prophesies revolved around King Henry VIII, his wife, Queen Catherine of Aragon, and the woman Barton called "the Bullen whore"—Anne Boleyn. "Bad stuff's gonna happen if you divorce queen number one!" she would yell.

When the palace got wind of her actions, Barton and others were arrested and thrown in the Tower of London. A few sessions with the latest dungeonside devices, and everyone sang Dixie, after which King Henry had them paraded to Canterbury to publicly confess. Then Henry and his aides decided what the heck, they could use this opportunity to get rid of some other tiresome Catholics. Seven people in all—twenty-five-year-old Barton included—were burned to death at Tyburn. Before she died, I wonder if the Holy Maid got an update from the spirit world—one that showed how miserable King Henry's life was going to be from that moment on?

WITH A SUITOR LIKE THIS, WHO NEEDS ENEMIES?

ometimes 'twas a far far better thing to have loved and lost a throne—especially if the throne in question was occupied by the hefty haunches of one Henry VIII of England. That's what **Christina of Denmark** thought, anyway. In 1538, Henry was spouse-hunting again, having lost wife number three to childbed fever. His globe-trotting artist Hans Holbein painted Christina's likeness—and the king loved it. As a bonus, this dimpled duchess, Danish by birth and already a duke's widow at sixteen, resembled **Madge Shelton**, the saucy intern at the English court who'd given Henry palpitations (or something) during the pregnancy of the late Queen Anne Boleyn.

Christina also loved hunting, card playing, and other Henry hobbies. As the icing on the Euromerger cake, she was the niece of Charles V, Holy Roman Emperor. The English ambassador began negotiations, telling the duchess that by marrying Henry "you'll be matched with the most gentle Gentleman that liveth; his nature so benign and pleasant, that I think till this day no man hath heard many angry words pass his mouth." Christina knew an O.J. tall tale when she heard it. "If I had two heads, I'd be happy to offer King Henry one of them!" was her possibly apocryphal but much-repeated reply.

NOT "THE MOOST HAPPI"
FOR LONG

A bewitching commoner named **Anne Boleyn** survived a slimily ambitious father, a bout of deadly sweating sickness (a disease that swept England in 1528), and even the birth of a royal child of the wrong sex, only to succumb to a marital fatality of the highest order. Possessed of charm, high intelligence, and spiritual courage, this Queen of England was dispossessed of her head by a sharp blow from an executioner's sword, just 1,084 days after her marriage to King Henry VIII.

For seven years, Anne's wily "no extracurricular sex with the king" campaign had kept the lusty, heir-mad monarch on the boil for her charms, while he worked on disengaging himself from Queen Catherine. Boleyn shoulda known better. The love didn't last. The thorny issue of succession reared its head, and Anne (whose portrait medal poignantly said "the Moost Happi") found that it took a male baby—and only a male—to satisfy Henry, not her snapping black eyes and other allures.

Although rarely credited with turning Henry into a Protestant, French-educated Anne unflinchingly did her best to bring him around to Lutheran views. Boleyn marked up passages in key religious books and made them required reading for Henry; she defended

Protestant extremists like William Tyndale, and brought his book to the king's attention; and she even intervened to save more obscure Protestant religious figures from punishment.

For her pains (and "her" disgraceful inability to pump out a viable male heir), Anne became very unpopular with the general public (many who'd never thought her marriage to Henry was valid, especially after the death of well-liked Catherine of Aragon). Add to that the backstage maneuverings of politicos, other people at court, and even members of her own family who had it in for miss fancy-pants nouveau queen, and even quick-witted Boleyn didn't stand a chance. Hers is the most tragic of the wives of Windsor stories; and the most graphic example of what a sick puppy the love-professing merry monarch really was.

Anne may have lacked a head at age twenty-nine; but she had the last laugh, historically speaking. Her long-lived daughter Elizabeth Tudor went on to become the monarch many think of as the most outstanding leader England has ever known.

FLANDERS MARE?
MORE LIKE DARK HORSE

Safe sex" was her middle name. Fourth wife and brief queen of scary Harry, what **Anne of Cleves** knew about the carnal act could have filled a thimble. Reared in a prudish household on the Rhine River in what is now Germany, Anne was pre-approved as a mate for Henry VIII from a portrait.

Her trip to England took forever. Once there, she was watching the puzzling torture of a bull from her window on New Year's Day when in popped a fat gent, tented in an unflattering multicolored cloak, who gave her a hug and a gift. *First, animal cruelty, and now this clown!* At a loss, Anne muttered a few epithets in German, and returned to the less embarrassing bull spectacle.

The fat gent scurried out, changed into regal gear and swooped back in, this time with attendants bowing, so Lady Anne would get the picture. Rough start to a royal relationship. By now, Henry was steamed because (1) Anne was "too serious," (2) not cute or charming, (3) poor at music and games. What really put him off, however, was her initial disinterest. At his age and weight, Henry needed the aphrodisiac of enthusiastic adoration.

He glumly went forward with the wedding. But when push came to shove, his bedside manner failed. The naive queen, on the other hand, thought things were going great. Asked to describe her sex life, she said, "When the king comes to bed, he kisses me and says 'goodnight sweetheart.'"

Henry has nerve, criticizing my hips. The man's as wide as he is tall.

With Henry hot for more male heirs, his lack of prowess had to be blamed on something. Aha! Anne's lack of sex appeal. Soon he found comfort in the arms of his next wife-to-be, Catherine Howard—and Anne found herself and her visa declared "invalid" after six months as Queen of England.

Ms. Cleves may have been a dud at games—but this time, she played her cards right. She gave in gracefully. Relieved, Henry made her a handsome settlement—as long as she remained in England. (Wouldn't do to have unflattering booty tales told back in Germany.)

Now independent, unmarried, and wealthy, Anne bought new clothes, took up gambling, gardening, pets, and had a stiff drink now and then. She made a point of becoming pals with Catherine, wife five, bringing her a "welcome to the Henry's Wives' club" gift of two horses dressed in matching mauve velvet. Still on the "A" list, Anne got invited to all the palace dos. At a banquet in 1541, when the king limped off to bed, she and Catherine even danced gaily together during the evening fete.

She outlived all of Henry's wives and him as well, and was buried with royal honors in Westminster Abbey in 1557—the only one of Henry's queens to be so recognized.

Tagged by history with the unkind description of "Flanders mare" (a jab incorrectly but often attributed to the king), Anne might justifiably be called "the dark horse," don't you think?

GREAT DAME IN THE FASHION DOGHOUSE

When hatters go bad (or mad): in the late 1400s, some twisted soul came up with the "gable" or "kennel" head-dress for women. Despite its hideousness, this heavily jeweled and embroidered fashion disaster was adopted by **Elizabeth of York,** English queen of Henry VII—quickly making it into the Jackie Kennedy pillbox of its day.

This Tudor royal rose did more than inflict the kennel on her people. In between card games (she was a fanatical player of this new indoor sport that was sweeping Europe), going shopping, and spending money on her sisters, Elizabeth produced eight heirs, including the Big One: the little redhead who grew (and grew, and grew) to become Henry VIII. Beloved by both her Henrys, Elizabeth got immortalized in an offbeat way: before her husband died, Henry VII stan-dardized the deck of English playing cards. On them, blonde Elizabeth was portrayed as "the Queen of Hearts." And there she remains today, in her kennel headdress, clutching a flowery symbol that originally represented the War of the Roses.

The kennel headdress: into the fashion doghouse.

247

making high-end art
for a high roller

ne of three artists in a talented Flanders family from Ghent (now in Belgium), **Susanna Hornebolt** specialized in manuscript illumination—spending most of her time illustrating, then painting and gilding collectors' editions of fancy, hand-calligraphed books and other pieces.

While still a teen and living with her family, Susanna's work caught the discerning eye of Germany's hottest artist, Albrecht Dürer, who was traveling through the Low Countries with his wife Agnes. He dropped by the Hornebolt studio, and ended up with one of the girl's pieces. Later he wrote a friend, "Susanna, the daughter of Master Gerard, has illuminated a Savior on a little sheet, for which I gave her one florin," adding with a teeth-grinding touch of condescending naiveté, "It's very wonderful that a woman can do so much!"

Dürer wasn't the only art professional to praise her. She won more whole-hearted compliments from Italy's most listened-to art critics, Vasari and Guiccardini (the Ren's Siskel and Ebert).

In 1528, the Hornebolts moved to England, drawn by the distinct possibility of working for the world's most materialistic royal—King Henry VIII. Right away, Susanna, her dad Gerard, and her brother Lucas got lucky. Henry, who collected palaces (fifty-five), tapestries (2,000), silverplate (2,028), and illuminated books (count-less), needed more. Susanna and her family began work on a series of deluxe religious books, official treaties, and other stuff for this collecting junkie. The high-fiving trio jubilantly saw they had work for a lifetime, limning the lavish gold-and-crimson books.

What with illuminating, and dashing off a few miniatures, Susanna probably didn't get out much. She didn't need to. As part of the entourage of King Henry's huge court (the head count went from five hundred to eight hundred people at court, depending on season), she had lots of company. That's probably where she met—and married—John Parker, a yeoman to the king. In later years, she wed a sculptor named Worsley, went to live in Worchester, and died in her forties "in wealth and honor," as one admiring critic put it.

NURSEMATE WANTED:
GOOD GROVEL A MUST

he sixth and last wife of Henry VIII, **Catherine Parr** survived him—even after disagreeing heartily with him. She was a foxy widow who'd been around the marital block a time or two before she got hitched to old Hal. By the time he wooed Parr, the king himself had high road miles (to say nothing of wife murders, puzzling illnesses, and megalomania). It all began in 1543. Catherine had just found a love hunk in Sir Thomas Seymour, when something big intervened—a bloated monarch with a fifty-inch waistline. Royal duty called, Parr decided.

For nearly four years, the new queen acted as Henry's nurse (he called her "Kate"), took in his children and reconciled him with them, and mostly kept mum about her female circle of learned women and her Lutheran leanings. Mostly. Once Parr piped up, and alarms went off; Henry ordered her arrested and her books audited. Luckily, Kate knew how to do an inspired job of groveling; by the time the king's guards showed up, she'd gotten back in the Blimp's good graces again.

Once King Henry was safely entombed, Catherine got two religious books published that she'd had a hand in, then treated herself to a real relationship and wed Thomas Seymour, the man she'd fallen for earlier. She soon found romance to be a rocky road. For all her wisdom, wealth, and good sense, Catherine flipped out with jealousy over the richly bearded, highly horny Thomas.

She also found herself pregnant at thirty-five—which inspired her hubby to begin morning foreplay sessions with a teenaged Princess Elizabeth, the future queen of England. Rather than object, on at least one occasion Catherine joined in. After this disturbing romp, she came to her senses and sent teen Elizabeth away—probably more for the girl's protection than for darker motives.

Like countless mothers before her, the life of this kindly and bright woman ebbed away in the aftermath of childbirth. She died in

September 1548; six months later, her idiotically ambitious husband Thomas got snarled in a conspiracy plot and lost his head. Little Mary Seymour, the orphaned baby daughter of Catherine and Thomas, melted away slowly, like a young ghost; her death in later childhood was not even noted in the records.

Stuck with the unlovely bratwurst King Henry of later years.

JUST DYING TO LEARN MORE

ll **Jane Grey** wanted was to be a humanist scholar—was that too much to ask? Yes, apparently. In the long history of English monarchs, Lady Grey was a blip on the radar screen, a queen for nine days, pushed into ruling because of her royal blood by the duke of Northumberland and other power players.

This granddaughter of Henry VIII's sister grew up in an abusive household. As a young girl, Jane wrote: "When I'm in the presence of father or mother, whether I speak, keep silence, sit, stand or go, eat, drink, be merry or sad, be sewing, playing, dancing, or doing anything else, I must do it . . . so perfectly as God made the world, else I am so sharply taunted, so cruelly threatened, sometimes with pinches, nipps, and bobs, and other ways (which I will not name for the honor I bear them), so without measure misordered that I think myself in hell."

Jane's only respite was her tutor, Mr. Aylmer; her only joy, that of learning. "Mr. Aylmer, who teacheth me so gently, so pleasantly with such fair allurements to learning, that I think all the time nothing while I am with him. And when I am called from him, I fall on weeping, because whatsoever I do else but learning, is full of grief, trouble, fear, and wholly misliking to me. And thus my book hath been so much my pleasure and more, that in respect of it, all other pleasures in very deed be but trifles and troubles unto me."

Too bad Jane couldn't stick to her Latin, Greek, French, and philosophy. But family ambitions sucked this sweet sixteen into the vortex. After Henry VIII died, the throne went to his ardently Protestant son Edward, who had tuberculosis. When those in power saw that the sickly teen was a goner, they cast about for a successor with royal blood and the right religion: up came Lady Jane Grey's name. With blinding speed, Jane was made to marry Guildford Dudley to reign with her, and the dying king changed the order of succession, so a Protestant queen could follow him on the throne.

Crowned at sixteen, Queen Jane was 1553's nine-day wonder. Her new husband and supporters weren't organized enough to pull off this coup, however. When Mary, Henry VIII's Catholic daughter and blood heir, arrived with an army, the whole pack of Greys were arrested for treason and got a group rate at the lockup in the Tower of London.

Just before she died by an executioner's ax, Jane gave her sister **Katherine** a New Testament as a going-away present. Inside she'd written: "It shall teach you to live, and learn you to die." Not surprisingly, the martyrdom of this brilliant and fanatically religious young humanist made Insta-queen Jane an icon to English Protestants.

Mary didn't fare much better as queen herself. Soon called "Bloody Mary" for her persecution of Protestants, she died of illness five years into her reign, about as popular as the plague.

THE PREGNANCY WAS VIRTUAL, THE CARNAGE WAS REAL

For a Catholic miss who couldn't wait to wed, things started looking good at age two. That's when **Mary I of England** sat in the arms of her godfather, Cardinal Wolsey, who slid a ring onto her finger and declared her the fiancée of the dauphin of France. Already eager for the delights of coupling, the precocious toddler said, "Are you the dauphin? If you are, I want to kiss you."

As the years wore on, and the dauphin deal fell through, and the number of Mary's proxy marriages rose, she started to get that "Always a fiancée, never a bride" feeling. By twenty-eight, this half-Spanish, half-English daughter of royals Catherine of Aragon and Henry VIII had the word *spinster* written all over her worried little face.

Time had its revenge, however. Mary outlived King Henry, all six of his wives, and his only male heir, her half-brother Edward, to become Queen of England. Ah-hah! she exulted, and turned to the most pressing affair of state: selecting her silver pattern and a suitable monarch to match.

She was wowed by one on the eligibles list: widower Philip II of Spain—Catholic as the pope, and a good looker too. In July 1554, despite scattered uprisings from a worried English populace, she married him at Winchester Cathedral. Soon Mary saw her waistline expand, and thought: A little Catholic heir! It was quite deflating when, months later, she began *deflating*. Dropsy rather than pregnancy was diagnosed; Philip, by now bored with her and the filthy English weather, became a long-distance husband.

Mary then decided that the problem with England was that it wasn't Catholic enough. Revving up the old heresy laws, she swung into action. The sale of firewood skyrocketed and human bonfires became a common sight. Now called **"Bloody Mary,"** the Queen frantically cremated Protestant big names and bishops alike.

Toasting a bishop or a cardinal wasn't so bad—what got locals inflamed were Mary's attacks on average Protestants—like blind Bible memorizer **Joan Waste.** (You can imagine the ill-natured press when Mrs. Waste had to be led to her bonfire.)

By 1558, Mary was ill, childless, all but bereft of her husband, and vilified by her own people. No place to go but up, right? Wrong: France now grabbed the city of Calais, England's last possession on the French mainland, and Mary took to her bed. On November 17, Londoners danced in the streets to cheer her demise—just as they'd done when she'd become queen, five years earlier. The burial was as schizophrenic as Bloody Mary herself; her corpse was buried at Westminster Abbey—her heart and bowels at St. James.

Trying to get ahead during Bloody Mary's regime.

TOMORROW DOESN'T LOOK GOOD, EITHER, YER MAJESTY

ften called "Mother," **Ursula Shipton** operated during the reign of King Henry VIII. Born about 1488 in a small cave in Yorkshire, she became one of London's most colorful characters, with a rep far and wide as a witch, a prophetess, and a seer or scryer. Need a look into the future? A love charm? A hate bracelet? Mother Shipton was your merchant of magick.

In Renaissance times, being identified as a witch was normally the best way to shorten your life span. Not so with Mother Shipton. She lived well into her seventies, a clairvoyant figure around whom popular legend swirled. And no wonder: even if her extrasensory powers were all showomanship, she was a weird-looking individual. Ursula had an unusually long head, fiery eyes, and a crooked nose, covered with what were described by awed contemporaries (including her husband) as "multi-colored phosphorescent warts."

The female Nostradamus of her day, Ursula Shipton aroused great excitement with her predictions regarding the fate of famous men and the end of the world (in her view, 1999 looked dreadful). Although she was probably illiterate, her fame endured for centuries, and accounts (mostly bogus) of her utterances continued to be published until the nineteenth century.

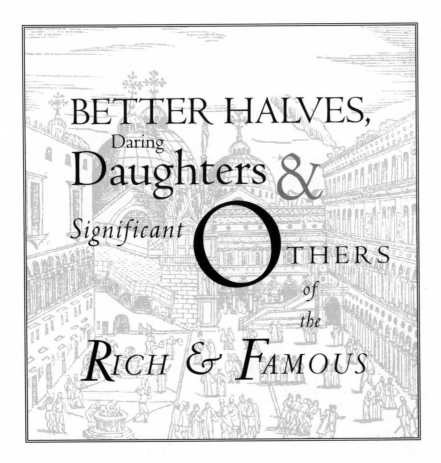

BETTER HALVES,
Daring
Daughters &
Significant Others
of
the
RICH & FAMOUS

LUTHER'S RIB & ANCHOR

Protestant rebel Martin Luther was in a quandary. His manifesto contained the radical idea that clergy should marry, and monks and nuns everywhere were saying, "Right on!" In 1523, the issue got personal. At Nimbschen convent, twelve nuns wanted to leave their cloister and asked for help. Sneaking even the slimmest nun out of a nunnery was tricky—UPS didn't pick up in the area.

But Martin pulled it off, orchestrating a Great Escape in herring barrels on a delivery wagon. He then found mates for everyone but **Katie von Bora.** Twenty-six-year-old Bora had brains and chutzpah; she leaned on Luther to find her a suitable spouse. "Someone like . . . oh, you, for instance," she hinted.

Luther was thunderstruck. "I'm not good husband material—gosh, I'll probably be burned at the stake in a year or two."

She persisted, though. And in 1525, the unromantic forty-two-year-old and Katie held a BYOBB (bring your own beer barrel) wedding party. Their marriage was a mutual admiration partnership, despite Martin's lack of earning power and personal habits. (Before Katie, he'd let a year go by before washing his bed sheets.) He called her "my lord Katie" and "my rib." Although Luther's earnings were slim, wealthy supporters gave them a recycled cloister as a home, and sent wine, food, and clothes at intervals.

Enterprising Katie developed her own orchard, garden, and fish pond, while doing the slaughtering, planting the fields, reading a Bible verse or two, and birthing six Luthers. She also made and sold great beer. At their home, she took in forty paying boarders and dozens of shirt-tale relatives. Katie loved the give-and-take at her dinner table, crowded with freeloading Protestant celebrities, religious refugees, and friends.

Although Martin Luther warned, "No good ever came out of female domination," he also learned about the sacred "honey-do" contract between a man and wife. As he wrote, "Get you a wife and then your mind, however fussy, will become straight as a ribbon. It will be reduced to one idea: Do and think as she wishes."

In the end, this oh-so-pragmatic marriage became a love match. As Martin said, "Katie, you have a husband that loves you. Let someone else be empress."

After Luther's death in 1546, Katie continued coping. Twice she and family had to flee invading armies, then rebuild. Then she suffered a driving accident and was thrown into a ditch. After months of illness, she died, saying, "I will stick to Christ as a burr to a topcoat."

The woman who housebroke Martin Luther.

A HOT FLASH FOR GALILEO'S SUNSET

either marriage nor miles kept **Alessandra Bocchineri** from conducting a virtual flirt with Galileo Galilei, Italy's famed celestial scientist. By her mid-thirties, La Bocchineri had dazzled royal courts at Mantua, Italy, and Vienna. These conquests seemed inadequate to Alessandra, who grumbled, "I have a mind, too, y'know." At length the merry widow took on her third mate, a Florence diplomat. What really excited the seasoned bride, however, was the news that she was now the sister-in-law of Galileo Junior—which made her kissing cousins with Galileo Senior.

Before long she and the elder Galileo were firing off letters, the seventy-seven-year-old from his villa, where he was under house arrest. Alessandra soon mooned for more than Mr. G. on paper. In a 1641 letter, she tantalized, "I often wonder how I'll be able before I die to find a way to be with you and spend a day in conversation without scandalizing or making those people jealous who have made fun of us for this wish." We don't know if she got her tête-à-tête. Galileo did, however, write the last communication of his life to her, saying, "Your letter is a great consolation, for I've been confined to bed for many weeks. . . . I beg you to excuse my involuntary brevity, and with most warm affection I kiss your hands."

BURNED BY FATE

y the time she'd been married to Nicholas Bacon for a bit, **Anne Cooke Bacon** was no doubt sick of jokes about her name. Because instead of cooking it, she was busy bringing *home* the bacon. Before and after bringing sons Francis and Anthony into the world in the mid-1500s, Anne worked as an author and a translator of religious works in Latin and Italian, turning fourteen Calvinist sermons and the official book for the Church of England into English. (Anne's sisters Katherine, Mildred, and Elizabeth were no slouches at writing and translation, either.)

Both of Anne's boys had homosexual leanings. Anthony kept a stable of what were called "wanton boys," was charged with sodomy, and wisely went to France to live. Her highbrow, high-profile son Francis became an essayist, scientist, and politician—and part of Queen Elizabeth's inner circle, despite her dislike of his gender preference. Later in life, Francis took political bribes, was convicted and lost his office, and ratted on lifelong friends. By good fortune, his mother didn't see his downfall, having died in 1610.

An Absentee Daddy's Girl

Famed astronomer Galileo Galilei could probably teach the current crop of deadbeat dads a thing or two about stop payments. While a lowly math prof in 1597, Galileo linked orbits with a Venetian gal named **Marina Gamba,** producing a son and two daughters. After ten years of liaison, Galileo took off, and Marina got left with *niente*—no palimony, no nothing. In view of how hot Galileo would become (the Inquisition threw him out of the church for his "heretical" views on the heavens), perhaps Ms. Gamba came out on the plus side.

Not a hands-on dad, either, Galileo stuck his daughters at his mom's, so he could spend time keeping the rest of his hapless family afloat. For instance, he went halvies on a dowry for his sister Livia, but his brother Michelangelo stiffed him, then borrowed more money—and moved to Poland. Mike played that fraternal trick several times before Galileo wised up.

Galileo's elder daughter, **Virginia Galilei,** seeing what a bozo her dad was at everyday finance, opted for the spiritual life and entered a convent at Arcetri in 1616. Already fond of her, Galileo grew positively affable when she became Sister Maria Celeste. She stood by him during his trial by Inquisition, his house arrest, and other tribulations, from scholarly attacks to hernias. Some of her communications still exist, revealing a loyal, sensitive, and intelligent young woman.

One of the most eloquent letters to survive from Renaissance times is in fact from Virginia, consoling her excommunicated dad. "Do not say that your name is struck 'from the book of the living,' for that is not so, either in the rest of the world or in your own country. Rather, it seems to me that if your name and reputation were briefly under a cloud, they are now restored to greater fame—which is astonishing, since I know that no one is accounted a prophet in his own land."

Her prescient remarks were realized the very next year, when the scientist's books were published in French and Latin, bringing Galileo's ideas to a huge new European audience. Tragically, 1634 also saw the jolt of Virginia's death in her early thirties. That loss, together with his condemnation by the Catholic Church, were blows from which Galileo never recovered.

NO NECK BITES ON MRS. DRAC

From 1462 on, **Ilona Szilagy** kept finding marriage proposals with a Transylvania postmark in her mailbox. First cousin of Hungarian King Matthias, Ilona belonged to the snooty Corvinus clan. The mystifying proposals were from sadist and social climber Vlad "my fiends call me Dracula" the Impaler, the prince of three measly provinces. Ilona was contemptuous; why, the man didn't even terrorize a real country! However, politics—or cousinly payback—intervened, and in 1467, King Matthias gave the green light for Ilona to wed the dread Vlad.

Dracula had to jump a few hoops to win his woman, being locked up in a castle, more political refugee than prince, at the time of the nuptials. Matthias made him promise to annihilate the invading Turks and convert to Catholicism. (However, Vlad did not have to give up his favorite leisure activities, such as nailing diplomats' hats to their heads.)

As a wedding gift, Matthias gave the couple a house in Pest: "right across the river from Buda—you can't miss it." Ilona settled in to procreate as Mrs. Dracula, and before long, several baby Dracs graced the premises.

In late 1476, Ilona had a tremendous stroke of luck: Mr. Impaler died in battle at age forty-five and soon had his own head displayed on a stake in Constantinople. Ilona moved back to Buda to enjoy *her* favorite leisure activity—succession intrigues. Eventually she saw her son on the Wallachian throne for a nanosecond, before the real bloodshed began among Drac descendants and would-be Vlads.

Some prince—he doesn't even terrorize a whole country.

265

home sweet cell

er birth-control timing may have been off, but her fashion timing was impeccable. In 1591, when **Bess Throckmorton** discovered there was a little Sir Walter Raleigh on the way, it was a snap to hide it. With the Elizabethan passion for underpinnings, like the farthingales that women wore on their hips, Bess could have hidden a 757 on her person and no one would have been the wiser—not even eagle-eyed Queen Elizabeth. As a lady-in-waiting to the queen, Bess had had to sign a "no dallying" document as a condition of employment.

Bess managed to time her vacation and birth a boy, returning to court with no one the wiser. She and Walt were secretly married by now—which made the whole thing much more heinous when the queen eventually found out. A dalliance, she could have overlooked. An illegitimate birth, forgiven. But marriage? Without her blessing? Thou art in deep doodoo indeed, asserted the queenly single. When Walter idiotically failed to beg forgiveness, the queen threw all three into the Tower of London. Walt wrote a pathetic poem to the queen and got sprung in a month; Bess and child remained imprisoned for half a year.

Mrs. Raleigh did manage to enjoy some married years at large, but Walt screwed up again during the next administration and got thrown into the Tower by King James for plotting treason with the Spaniards, a phony charge to get him out of circulation. Although Walt had a death sentence pending, he had conjugal visit privileges. Eventually, faithful Bess was allowed to move into his rather ample jail digs. The couple had another son, then brought in a few servants. Pretty soon Bess was whipping up canapés for drop-ins and celebrity visitors. When not entertaining, Sir Walter kept busy in a makeshift lab, dreaming up over-the-counter remedies.

By 1616, the political climate had changed, and the Raleigh family finally got out of lockup. The king gave the aging Walt a sexy new assignment: Find El Dorado! With unerring incompetence, Sir Walter got into a fight with Spanish explorers also looking for El Dorado. Walt had brought along their son Wally, who was killed in the melee. As he wrote to Bess: "I ne'er knew what sorrow meant until now. My brains are broken, and 'tis a torment for me to write. If I live to return, it is the care for you that hath strengthened my heart."

Raleigh returned to England and his fed-up wife, only to receive the unkindest cut of all—a very ticked-off monarch who decided to impose that long-ago death sentence, and had Sir Walter beheaded.

Hooray for farthingales—the next best thing to birth control.

BEHIND WILL'S WILL

For centuries, Shakespeare fans have reveled in the plays and love sonnets of the Elizabethan genius. But few recall what a crumb Will was to his wife, **Anne Hathaway**. In his will, he inserted a rude P.S., leaving Anne "the second-best bed." Was this a commentary on their love life? Or a sarcastic code word for a more loving interlude?

No matter how much leeway we allow Shakespeare, Anne lived much of their married life as a single mom. Pregnant when they married in 1582, Anne (also known as Agnes) Hathaway was twenty-six to his eighteen years. Their first daughter **Susanna** was born on May 26, 1583. Two years later, the Shakespeares had twins: **Judith** and **Hamnet**, conceived during a quickie commute to Stratford perhaps, and named after family friends. At this point, Will was already living and working in London; by 1590, he'd written his first play. Although she would outlive Shakespeare, little else is known about Anne—except the location of the thatched Stratford cottage where she grew up, still a must-see for dewier-eyed tourists.

But what about Shakespeare's quote, real love—the woman of his tortured sonnets? Thought to be written during a period when a bad bout of the plague closed the London theaters, Will's sonnets run the gamut from sublime ("Let me compare thee to a summer's day") to rancid (sonnet 151, called the "gross sonnet" because its central image is the rise and fall of the poet's phallus). Heavy-breathing historians speculate endlessly about Shakespeare's "Dark Mistress," but it's altogether possible that Will conducted his affair from the sidelines.

Among the top femmes fatales in the running for the Dark Lady was **Emilia Bassano.** A lush Italian minx and the daughter of court musicians, she hooked up with Lord Chamberlain Hunsdon. When she got pregnant in 1592, he skillfully married her to a musician named Lanier.

Another Dark Lady contender was **Mary Fitton,** an aristocratic beauty with a widow's peak and a spicy reputation, the mistress of the earl of Pembroke and the queen's maid of honor. Fitton had several children out of wedlock, later marrying into the Newdegate family.

No amount of research has yet placed either Fitton or Bassano in Shakespeare's bed, second-best or otherwise. In 1609, however, after the unauthorized publication of Shakespeare's sonnets, Emilia Bassano published a poem of her own that (among other topics) ripped into men who wrote derogatory poetry about women. Not conclusive evidence, but the timing is provocative.

When you get right down to it, Shakespeare's Dark Lady could be imaginary—or a composite of various women who'd rung his chimes through the years. After all, that's what a genius of a playwright and poet works with best: his imagination.

POSTMORTEM BLISS
IN OLD PORTUGAL

nce Spanish lady-in-waiting **Inés de Castro** had learned to kowtow properly, there wasn't much excitement to her job. But what's this? Portugal's biggest marital catch, Pedro the First, was headed their way, to woo her princess. To get her vicarious thrills, Inés hung around to see the princely assets. Despite his betrothal, Portuguese Pete took one look at this señorita—and love alarms went off. On both sides. What with propinquity and poor castle lighting, Inés and Pedro found it easy to rendezvous—but not so easy to keep their chat room private.

Pretty soon, Pete's dad, King Alfonso, was on their case. Love and/or lust would not prevail, he thundered, and banished Inés to some godawful place, like the Costa del Sol. For five years, Inés languished while Pedro endured marriage to the princess. In 1345, she got an e-mail from him: "You-know-who now RIP. Let's meet ASAP." Inés dashed to Coimbra, where she and Petie had a passionate reunion, culminating in El Niño (or possibly two).

Even though Pedro was officially a widower, King Alfonso just wouldn't quit meddling in his son's life. Worried that Pedro and that vile upstart Inés were secretly married and producing half-Spanish upstarts to his throne, in 1355 he sent a goon squad to do her in. Their lethal weapons hacked the poor woman into paella-sized pieces.

Shattered by Inés' death, Pedro brooded until his dad expired—then the new king had the assassins' hearts ripped out of their chests in his presence. Having quickly earned the nickname "the Cruel," King Pedro wondered what else could he do to honor his lost love. Build a cathedral? Boring. Dedicate a convent? Too predictable.

At last he thought of a fitting tribute. Although Inés had been taking a dirt nap for five years, Pedro had her dug up, dressed in crown and robes, and propped next to him on the golden throne of Portugal. Then he ordered the members of his court to pay her homage. Everyone could see that King Cruel wasn't operating on all cylinders by now. One by one, they approached the throne, and on Pedro's orders, kissed what was left of the hand of Inés, while trying not to inhale.

This fearsome display of true love became an inspiration (or a warning) for generations of poets. Inés de Castro and Pedro are still together, incidentally, reposing at a Portuguese monastery in a double-wide tomb, considered the best funerary sculpture ever.

YEARS WOULD HAVE BEEN
BETTER THAN GUILDERS

When this girl with hair like a shower of golden coins sat for Rembrandt van Rijn in 1634, **Saskia van Ulenborch** charmed the homely painter right out of his chair. After two sittings, he proposed—and Saskia said, "Yes." The orphaned daughter of a well-fixed judge, Miss van Ulenborch was well-padded physically and fiscally. Both as his model and his love, Saskia brought him tremendous happiness—and her dowry assets let him indulge his penchant for costumes, art, jewelry, stock shares, and real estate to a careless extent.

They had four children; after each, Saskia faded a little, especially when three died young. A few weeks before her thirtieth birthday, Rembrandt's wife, now dying of an unknown disease, made her will. She left her money to their surviving son Titus, and the interest on it to her husband, while the boy was still a minor. If Rembrandt remarried, he and Titus got nothing. (A slap on the hand from beyond the grave?) What Saskia didn't foresee was that her husband would sink further into debt, and lose clients, rather than the other way around.

Rembrandt was exceedingly fortunate in his loves. If it hadn't been for the big heart of **Hendrickje Stoffels,** his second significant other, this genius at painting (and flop at finance) might well have ended up in debtors' prison.

REN WOMEN'S BEST-KEPT FASHION SECRET

ew women have had their wedding portrait painted by a Flemish master like Jan van Eyck, but **Giovanna Cenami** did. The young bride of Lucca Arnolfini, an anorexic Italian merchant in a goony hat, she's usually called "the bride" or "the betrothed" of Arnolfini. Maybe that anonymity is a blessing—given that Giovanna appears to be heavily pregnant.

If premarital chastity was such a hot-button issue in 1434, how come Cenami looks ready to pop? Simple. Giovanna was flaunting fashion, not fertility. Her green skirts that billowed front and center were *le dernier cri.* To achieve the look, women stuffed their underwear with cotton pads to protrude even further. Call it B.B.: the Big-Belly Look for Spring—he'll love your Virgin Mary glow! All those Renaissance paintings you've puzzled over, showing gals who look like they should be in the birthing room, not an artist's studio? Mystery solved. Given that Giovanna and her contemporaries often *were* pregnant, the B.B. look was both comfortable and hip. Looking expectant all the time hopelessly confused husbands as well, and provided a much-needed form of birth control in a day when "I've got a migraine" just didn't cut it. Makes you wonder, though, why were women persuaded to move on to rib-deforming bodices and other torture devices?

AT LEAST SHE HAD
HER PRINTS CHARMING

ome artists' wives had all the luck. Take **Agnes Dürer**, the solid and stalwart wife of Albrecht. Not only was her husband an enormous talent, the guy was a hunk. (Agnes felt so relieved—she could have ended up with a weirdo like Michelangelo. Or that El Greco character.)

As the fifteen-year-old daughter of a well-to-do metal worker, Agnes Frey brought a healthy dowry of two hundred florins to the Dürer enterprise. In fact, her new husband dipped into it shortly after marriage, to finance an extended art trip to Italy. She wasn't too thrilled to be left with her parents, and in the middle of a plague outbreak yet.

Still, unlike some starving artists she could name, hers wasn't. In fact, Al was pretty sharp when it came to marketing himself. As the years rolled by, he published thousands of his own etchings and prints, made right in the workshop on the first floor of their gorgeous five-story house.

Agnes had to do a lot of the sales legwork—not that she wasn't glad to. Every morning, there she was at her stall in the Nuremberg marketplace or the Frankfurt fair, flogging his prints to the public. As Al said, she handled the money end of things very competently.

Once in awhile (a *great* while), she even got a trip out of the deal. The summer of 1521, for instance, when Al took her on a nice year-long excursion from Nuremberg to the Netherlands for their twenty-sixth anniversary. They stayed in inns, or sometimes were entertained by friends. (No cooking!) Al, now in his fifties, took it easy, did a few silverpoint or charcoal portraits, including one of her in a hat he bought for her in Brussels. It was a real treat to put her feet up and dish with the maid for a change.

The only down side to marrying a Dürer were those darned portraits Al drew of her. She hated what they now showed: an aging housewife with discontent written on her face, a woman with no children and a husband whose intellectual life and closest friends were in another galaxy. Come to think of it, maybe it was some other artists' wives who had all the luck.

Even after becoming a widow, Agnes got criticized in the meanest way by Al's hoity-toity humanist friends, all of them claiming, "Ya ya! Al meant for me to have that etching as a gift!" Agnes didn't care if they call her "grasping" and "jealous" in their writings; she wasn't about to give Al's work away—it was all she ever had.

It was the pits, being Al's model.

275

CHIP OFF
THE OLD CROMWELL

The spitting image of her grandfather, famed Puritan and Roundhead rebel Oliver Cromwell, **Bridget Bendish** caused shivers—and not just of nostalgia—for the good old days of 1653–1658, when Cromwell as Lord Protector had ruled England with a dictatorial hand.

Born about 1649 to Cromwell's daughter Biddy, the girl child hung around her grandfather, cosseted by him until his death when she was nine or so. Thus Bridget saw herself in the catbird's seat as the official Cromwell "That's the Way it Was" historian.

A woman passionate about history, Bridget was known to draw a sword if any unwary person in her presence hocked up a slighting remark about Grandpa. She considered him "next to the twelve apostles, the first saint in heaven"—an opinion shared by few, even in Ollie's lifetime.

Fortunately, she didn't get many arguments down on the salt pans, where she and husband Thomas Bendish owned farmland and a large salt works with a nice mansion set in its midst. Bridget liked to do her own household chores—even the physical labor of hauling the salt. Dressed in a battered straw hat, grubby clothes, and no underwear, she would get down and dirty with her workmen, "insensible to all the necessities and calls of nature, and in appearance beneath the meanest of them," according to a lifelong friend.

An omnivorous but not fastidious eater and drinker, Bridget knocked back anything that was put in front of her. When a grand occasion arose, however, she could match black silk dresses and dainty manners with the finest gentry.

As she grew older, Bendish became a widow and even more of a dervish, staying up very late, calling on friends at 10 P.M. and staying until the early hours, vivaciously laughing and drinking up all the wine in sight. Only then would she leave, mounted on an old mare, and singing into the night.

Generous to a fault, rapturously religious, and politically adventuresome, Bridget got herself into various scrapes, plots, and business disasters—but still thrived. In her old age, she resembled Oliver Cromwell more and more, right down to the warts on her face. She got excited about cattle-grazing, and took to traveling to the cattle fairs on her own—an independent old spirit to the last and a delightful, if shocking, model for female indecorum.

FETA WORSE THAN DEATH?
NYET!

he final shred of DNA from the Byzantine royal line, **Zoe Palaiologina** was the niece of the last Christian emperor of Constantinople. In 1460, Zoe and kin even got chased out of their remaining city of Mistra, located in a nowhere part of southern Greece.

For awhile, the refugees hid out in Rome, as guests of the pope. Their harassed host was way behind on his convert quota for the quarter. Then the Holy Father looked at Zoe, still going through the heartbreak of puberty, and thought: Merger time! If Russia's top man, Ivan III, won the hand of the very last Byzantine heiress in a nonhostile takeover, then surely as their part of the bargain, the Russians would convert to Catholicism (thus giving the pope some excellent new numbers for his next quarter).

Going to his petty cash fund, the pope came up with an attractive bride-plus-dowry package, then carefully negotiated a deal with the always-touchy Russians.

Zoe of course had the traditional "no say at all" in the arrangement. However, once away from the deal-closer, Zoe and Ivan shared a chuckle at the pope's religious presumption and in 1472, celebrated their wedding *their* way—in traditional Byzantine Orthodox style.

Now called Sophia, or Zoe Sophia, or Sophia Zoe by the moniker-crazy Russians, the sixteen-year-old suddenly remembered that she'd brought along a clutch of Italian architects. The pope had sent them as a wedding gift, hoping to revamp Moscow to match his exciting new tourist slogan: "the third Rome."

Zoe promptly put Italian hands to work on the decaying kremlin, or fortress complex, and magic happened. When finished, the new kremlin had eighteen slender towers and flowing walls, topped with soft-serve swirls and cones in rich shades of vanilla, butterscotch, and Neopolitan. The extravagant banana split of architecture is still Russia's major tourist attraction..

Zoe also had a major influence on fashion, court ceremonial, and customs, thanks to her entourage of Byzantine officials, flunkies, servants, and designers. She also occupies an odd footnote in history. Her husband, the first Russian ruler to style himself "czar" (after the Roman Caesar), became known as "Ivan the Great." After Zoe became the grandmother of another Ivan who decided to specialize in cruelty, she ended up with an "Ivan the Terrible" as well.

STAND BY YOUR VERTICALLY
CHALLENGED MAN

ueen-to-be **Henrietta-Maria** had guts—and good sea-legs. During her stormy Channel crossing, she kept writing letters, scornfully commenting, "Queens of England are never drowned."

However, when this French royal saw her stammering intended, Charles I, it was loath at first sight. Charlie had tics that would drive a nun to nicotine. She couldn't help looking down on her bridegroom—all four feet, ten inches of him. (And now we know why high-heeled shoes and stovepipe hats became high fashion in Charles' reign.) The aloof king wasn't all that taken with her, either. At fifteen, she was still on the scrawny, buck-toothed side.

Henrietta-Maria soon gave Charles a taste of her independent spirit. She shined on English lessons, preferring to gossip in French with her ladies-in-waiting. An ardent Catholic, she went to Mass, then disrupted Anglican church services at the palace by running a pack of hunting beagles through the room. The king was not amused, and cut off Henrietta's charge cards and painting lessons pronto.

It finally took a crisis—the assassination of Charles' right-hand man—to bring this troubled couple together. Demoralized, the tiny king turned to his diminutive wife for comfort and, first thing you know, they were in love and sleeping together. From 1628 on, despite a spinal deformity, Henrietta stayed pregnant nonstop. Those were the great years, a Norman Rockwell wallow of family gatherings (nine kids survived) and beautiful court theatricals or masques in which Henrietta took part as an actress. In fact, her first role in a pastoral drama made her the first actress in England.

No slacker when it came to gender parity, the queen also saw to it that other females besides her daughters got education in England—including the establishment of schools for commoners, not just the elite.

Meanwhile, a growing number of English became Frenchie-phobic, Catholic-loathing Puritans. And in 1642, England went to war with itself over how the country was to be governed. Barely over postpartum blues and only allowed one carry-on (she chose the baby), Henrietta-Maria set sail for France, where her exile would last for years. Charles, now in prison, wrote passionate letters in a secret cipher. Henrietta responded eagerly, thinking: *"Merde alors*—so *this* is, 'ow you say, birth control!"*

All too soon, however, the Parliamentarian forces, a.k.a. the Roundheads, detached King Charles' head from his body. His execution in

The Channel didn't turn her stomach—but the executioner did.

1649 got such rave reviews (What dignity! What courage!) that royalist stock among the English public soared.

Finally reunited with her children but not her man, Henrietta-Maria bit her lip and went on, as her sons spent years trying to invade England. It wasn't until the English got a taste of rule under Oliver Cromwell's son, the dopey kid everyone called "Tumbledown Dick," that the cry for "Bring back the royals!" became a roar.

In 1660, Henrietta's son Charles II landed at Dover to take the English throne. *Tout suite,* he set up his *maman* with the Jackie Kennedy special: a lavish house, an income of 60,000 pounds, and the best seats in the house at the two newly opened theaters.

MORE OF YOU TO LOVE

For the longest time, **Cecilia Vecelli,** a barber's daughter, played house with Tiziano Vecelli, a genial man later known to art history majors as Titian. Cecilia's man adored female flesh; the more avoirdupois, the merrier, was his motto. What with pasta three times a day, and the birth of two sons, and putting on a few kilos here and there—especially there—Cecilia and her rosy haunches remained Titian's favorite model. Although she might have been called "Mrs. Vecelli" out of courtesy at her local grocery store in Venice, it wasn't until the birth of her daughter that Tiziano popped the question. Mr. Romance even brought in a priest to preside and a goldsmith to make her a ring on the spot. Too bad new mom Cecilia couldn't enjoy it properly—she was on her death bed. Her gorgeous glowing flesh is still with us, however, in some of Titian's most luscious nudes.

MAMA NEEDS A
NEW PAIR OF SHOES

Daybreak to dusk, **Cecilia Guardi** worked her buns off, raising nine kids and cleaning up after her husband Giambattista Tiepolo and her two brothers, all well-known painters in Venice. She could cope—as long as she got a little evening action to cheer her up.

Soon, though, Cecilia's visits to the Ridotto casino became a nightly affair. What's the big deal, she argued, when confronted by her testy husband. It's only gambling. I can quit anytime!

At the Ridotto, everyone, rich or poor, was welcome in the plush red-and-gold rooms. Surrounded by gamble-happy Venetians, all in festive masks, Cecilia continued to be a random chance abuser. The day came when Mrs. G had a losing streak—a *long* losing streak. When the casino bosses found out she was flat out of ducats, Cecilia faced the final degradation: she had to sneak in a few of her spouse's drawings to pay off her debts.

Mrs. Guardi wasn't the only big loser; during and after the Renaissance, so many families in Venice went bankrupt over Ridotto mania that the place was shut down by the government in 1774.

short take

Better Halves,
Daring Daughters
& Significant Others
of the Rich & Famous

The trouble with being a maid to one of those bratty little Spanish princesses was that they'd walk all over you, given the chance. Especially in the case of **Maddalena Ruíz,** court dwarf. But the half-liter-sized career servant took it in stride. As the companion of the Infanta Isabella Clara Eugenia, one of the cutest Hapsburg princesses of the late 1500s, Maddalena was called on to run a few errands, make the princess laugh from time to time, and keep the royal lapdogs from messing on the best carpets. As she would say, it's a living.

Maddalena was a member of the royal household for decades, and a favorite of Clara's parents, Queen Elizabeth of Valois and King Philip II. Like most Spaniards, Maddie was fond of wine. Too fond, perhaps. As Philip once wrote to Clara: "Maddalena has been ill for some time. She's been purged and is still in a bad temper. . . . I think all this comes from what she drinks. . . ."

Cosseted Maddalena got medical attention whenever she took ill. Of course, in those days, getting near a doctor could kill you quicker than anything. Judging by the number of bleedings and purges Maddalena got, they didn't improve her health—or her temper. However, the petite Ruíz would probably brighten up to learn that she lives on in Velasquez' masterpiece, *Las Meninas,* one of the biggest crowd-pleasers at Madrid's Prado Museum.

SIB REVELRY,
NOT RIVALRY

An Irish lass with cerebellum to match her wit, **Sister Ranelagh** typified countless Renaissance women who, unconcerned about glory, credit, or career moves, concentrated on making the lives around them happy—and in turn, finding joy.

Baptized Katherine Boyle in 1614, she was one of ten in the raucous brood of the earl of Cork. Although her sister Mary defiantly wed for love, Katherine signed on for an arranged marriage at age fourteen with alcoholic Lord Ranelagh. When she wasn't putting her comatose husband to bed, she brought forth three daughters and a son, and kept mum about the lack of love (or even consciousness) in her marriage. Her siblings called her "Sister" all her life, and gradually so did everyone else. She had a natural gift for socialization; in fact, others called her "the best company in which to be merry."

At length, Sister Ranelagh and the kids left her drunken nobleman and came to England to live with her brother Robert Boyle for the next forty years. The sibs became a closer, more loving couple than many marrieds.

In the 1640s, famous poet John Milton became their neighbor—and Sister's close friend in the platonic sense. (Well, *possibly* platonic:

in 1643, Milton's first wife, Mary Powell, left him after one month of marriage.) Besides hanging out with Milton and other eggheads, Sister had a terrific verbal memory and often wrote down sermons verbatim. In her forties, she took up Experimental Philosophy and the study of Hebrew.

Sister Ranelagh also became the neighborhood connection for a growing array of medicines (quack and otherwise). In those gloriously unregulated times, Robert (known today as "the Father of Modern Chemistry") spent ages in his lab, whipping up weird compounds and inventing things. Once Father and Sister had figured out what they might be good for, Katherine handed them out free to ailing friends and neighbors. In this fashion, most of the wealth the two Boyles had inherited trickled away. (Given the high probability of accidental poisoning, some of the friends and neighbors may have trickled away, too.)

There were other showers on Katherine Boyle's parade. Her children were a grievous disappointment—especially one hussy of a daughter who ran off with the footman, later producing a baby out of wedlock. Troubles notwithstanding, she and her brother lived into their eighties together. In 1691, when the woman that Robert called "his dearest sister and constantly obliging friend" died, he followed just one week later.

ḃer smarts got Rembrandt off the ḃook

ike many painters, Rembrandt van Rijn was a Dutch master at the "I'm just so bad with money" schtik. Luckily, he had a gal pal in a million: the redoubtable **Hendrickje Stoffels.** After becoming a widower, Mr. R. played house with his son's nanny, who brought a breach-of-promise suit. Stoffels stepped in, giving testimony that got him off the marital hook. She took on the job of mothering his small son Titus, later becoming that staple of starving artists, the muse/model/mistress. In 1654, she shyly announced, "A little artist is on the way," hoping to get a more binding offer. Instead, she got slammed with a fine and public repentance for "the sin of fornication" by church authorities. Rembrandt, in dire need of the income stream from his late wife's will, refused to remarry. With a sigh, Hendrickje had baby Cornelia, and kept on modeling and keeping house for the guy.

Although it might seem hard to see how Rembrandt's financial situation could have worsened, in 1658, it did. The painter went bankrupt; the $65,000 house he'd bought with first wife Saskia, the antiques, the art, were auctioned for a pittance. At this point, problem-solver Hendrickje went into partnership with seventeen-year-old Titus. In an artful ploy that would move the IRS to tears, their enterprise shielded Mr. R. from his creditors while allowing him to work as an "employee" of the H&T art dealership. Thanks to mistress and son, Rembrandt had breathing room to produce his most powerful works.

With this kind of stress, it's no wonder Hendrickje died young. At least, however, our single mom and volunteer stepmom left a legacy that few could top: a series of exquisite paintings of her by Rembrandt, who clearly did love this woman who shared his life for twenty years. The surviving paintings, including *Woman Bathing in a Stream,* are considered by many to be the most touching works in the artist's huge oeuvre.

PETE'S SIS WAS
PRETTY GREAT, TOO

A French ambassador to **Sophia of Russia**'s court once sniffed, "She's immensely fat, with a head as large as a bushel, hairs on her face, and tumors on her legs." Not completely suicidal, he added: "Although her body is short and coarse, her mind is shrewd, unprejudiced, and full of policy. She's never read Machiavelli but she understands his maxims exactly."

If she chose to, Sophia could probably have written *The Prince*. The sister of various male heirs, she was born way down the food chain of successors to the Russian throne. Stuck in the Kremlin version of a harem, as all little czarinas were, Sophia oozed her way into a decent education, sopping up foreign languages and classes on dirty politics with her brother Alex. When Alex died, followed by her mom, Sophia's school days came to a screeching halt. Dad soon remarried, only to expire in 1676.

That's when hostilities between families one and two really flamed up. After feeble Fedor, the kid brother, took the throne, Sophia pushed her way in as his devoted nurse. Soon she got every pesky member of family number two sent to sunny Siberia—a nicely Machiavellian performance for a nineteen-year-old.

Sophia didn't even break a sweat over her next power move: getting herself promoted to Czarina Number One, where she was well placed to take over when Fedor duly died—leaving just two small male heirs. After a messy bloodbath on the Kremlin's Red Stairway (and now we know how it got its name), Sophia was proclaimed Big Piroshski for the youngsters. One was her brother Ivan, unkindly nicknamed "sad head" for his tendency to throw epileptic fits. The other was her half-brother Peter—the czar who eventually came to be called "the Great."

For seven years, Sophia ran the roost, keeping the palace guard happy, putting various lovers, married and unmarried, into key posts, and throwing your usual despotic tantrums. She had the boy czars sit on dual thrones, while (legend has it) she fed them their lines from behind a curtain. Finally Sophia dispensed with coyness and just called the shots as *gosudarynya* or sovereign.

*No way am I signing up
for weekly electrolysis!*

For a despot, Sophia did a lot of good; she lowered taxes, improved fire prevention, raised literacy, and reorganized the army. She even managed to lower (temporarily) the drunkenness rates—a first for Russia. The czarina had a farsighted take on women's legal rights, legislating many improvements. Sophia, who disdained lip waxing but loved a bit of blusher, didn't go for the Russian "Keep 'em curtained" line. She and her female entourage often appeared unveiled in public and at church.

But all good despots, even Russian ones, must come to an end. Sophia's curtain call came in 1689, when Peter got old enough to shave. The two clashed publicly—then sly Sophia floated an assassination rumor that scared Peter so badly that he jumped out of bed in the middle of the night and ran naked into the forest.

Six confrontations, plots, counterplots, and rebellions later, Sophia entered a comfortable nunnery of her choice. Even then, she couldn't quite give up politics. At her encouragement, in 1698 a rebel group launched a coup to return her to the throne. It took Peter absolutely weeks to torture, kill, and drape the dead rebels outside Sophia's convent window, where they created quite a stench for some time to come.

THE GREAT
MADONNA ESCAPE

n the Prato district of Florence lived a young woman well endowed with worldly and physical assets by the name of **Lucrezia Buti.** The daughter of a local merchant, in 1455 Lucrezia was a nun junior grade at the convent of Santa Margherita when the big news hit: the nunnery had snagged none other than talented painter Fra Filippo Lippi to do the panel for their main altar!

Lippi, a monk whose talents at womanizing equaled those with the brush, had just started work when he caught a glimpse of a delicious body. Dazzled by Lucrezia's face and form, he hammered on the nuns until they allowed him to use her as a model for the Madonna in his altarpiece. Sure enough, he not only got Buti on canvas, he captured her heart—and other portions of her anatomy.

Lippi's normal M.O. was kiss-and-run, but Lucrezia won his heart as well. They schemed to elope. To break the young nun out, they needed a diversion. Fortunately, a fabulous new relic had just hit town: the authentic Girdle of Our Lady. Everyone, especially the nuns, would be there for the gala cathedral opening.

Like a virgin: Ex-nun models for two generations of painters.

293

It was a full house, except for Lucrezia, who made a clean getaway with Fra Filippo—leaving her dad grinding his teeth and the nuns of Santa Margherita in disgrace. Did the two care? Not a whit. Although Lippi merrily continued to enjoy a series of affairs throughout his life, Lucrezia remained his mate and occasional model.

In 1457, the couple had a son, named Filippino or "Little Phil." Finally, with some lobbying from bigwig Cosimo de Medici, one of Lippi's patrons, the pope relieved Lucrezia and Filippo of their by-now more than moot vows of chastity, and let them marry.

Lippi's fame extended to his pupils. One of the finest was a kid nicknamed Botticelli or "Little Barrel"—although he was slim as a rail. Unlike his teacher, Botticelli didn't revel in women, except as models. In fact, after well-meaning patrons tried to talk him into marriage, he had a nightmare about taking a wife, later saying, "I was so struck with grief that I woke up, and so as not to fall asleep again and dream of it once more, I got up and wandered up and down Florence all night like a madman." (Clearly a commitment phobia there.) In turn, "Little Phil," the son of Lucrezia and Lippi, became Botticelli's serious student. Judging by the similarities of the heavy-lidded, voluptuous-lipped Madonnas painted by Lippi, Botticelli, and Filippino, beauteous Lucrezia may have served as artistic inspiration for all three.

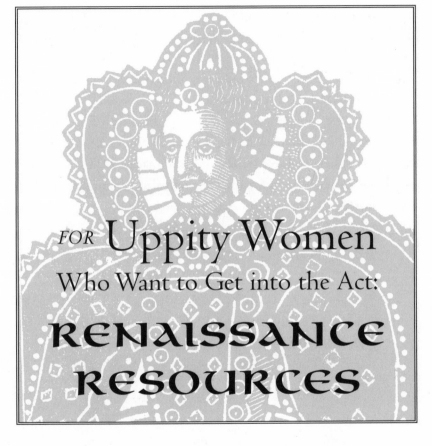

FOR Uppity Women
Who Want to Get into the Act:

RENAISSANCE
RESOURCES

WANT TO KICK UP your heels as a brazen medieval hussy or a Tudor trollop? Or how about taking on the persona of one of the outrageous trailblazers in this book? Take part (or be a spectator) in hundreds of annual events, from Renaissance Faires, Shakespeare Festivals, and Living History events to SCA (the Society for Creative Anachronism) activities across the United States, Canada, and in countries from England to Iceland.

Because phone numbers, addresses, and dates change often in our busy world, please use these listings as a jumping-off place. For more timely and detailed information, get the magazines listed below, phone the numbers given for specific groups and events, and contact the Websites and email addresses listed below.

- *Renaissance* Magazine (quarterly), 13 Appleton Road, Nantucket, MA 02554; E-mail: RenZine@aol.com
- *Renaissance Herald* (quarterly tabloid), P. O. Box 422, Riverside, CA 92502-0422; E-mail: reninfo@microsys.net
- *Tournaments Illuminated* (quarterly for SCA members), 1721 South Main Street, Milpitas, CA 95035
- *Living History* Magazine (quarterly, aimed largely at American history buffs and Civil War reenactors), P. O. Box 77, Fairfax, VA 22030; E-mail: 72774.2240@compuserve.com

The Society for Creative Anachronism, Inc. P. O. Box 360789, Milpitas, CA 95036; (408) 263-9305. Founded in 1966 and intended for participants rather than spectators, SCA has over 30,000 members worldwide (including England, Ireland, Scotland, Spain, Sweden, Finland, Germany, Belgium, Iceland, and the Netherlands). SCA is organized geographically by kingdoms and principalities, and at the local level by baronies, shires, colleges, or cantons. In the summer, SCA holds tournaments with jousting and overnight camping in period-style tents or pavilions. At other times of year, SCA members get together in costume for feasts or revels, calligraphy, medieval games, fencing, and a wide range of other medieval interests.

Renaissance Faires are festivals, large and small, usually held annually (often on successive weekends in warm weather) in locales across the United States, Canada, and elsewhere. For online information, use the Yahoo! search engine, followed by key words "Renaissance Faires" to access the listings; many faires have their own Web pages. Enter "North American Renaissance Faires" to access more material on over 100 faires or check the Websites and their multiple links:

- http://www.renaissance-village.com/
- http://www.renaissanceinfo.com/main.html
- http://www.panix.com/~wlinden/rennfair.html
- http://renstore.com/plaza/hotfairs.shtml
- http://www.njkingdom.com/links.html
- http://www.cygnus.com/~meissner/ren.html
- http://applink.net/wolfpack/faire.html

- http://renfaire.com/General/faire.html
- http://renstore.com/articles/fairlist.html
- http://www.georgetown.edu/labyrinth/subjects/women/women.html
- http://angelfire.com/mi/spanogle/medieval.html

SHAKEPEARE FESTIVALS

Shakespeare Festivals are held in Ashland, Oregon; Bloomington, Illinois; Saskatoon, Saskatchewan, Canada; and other locales each year. In Sherwood Forest, England, a huge annual Robin Hood Festival attracts over 250,000 attendees each year.

- Oregon Shakespeare Festival, Box 158, Ashland, OR 97520; (541) 482-4331
  http://www.orshakes.org., http://www.mind.net/osf/
- Illinois Shakespeare Festival, Campus Box 5700, Normal, IL 61790-5700. (309) 438-2535
  http://www.orat.itstu.edu/shakespeare
- Shakespeare on the Saskatchewan Festival in Saskatoon, Tourism Saskatchewan, 500-1900 Albert Street, Regina, Saskatchewan, Canada S4P 4L9; 800-567-2444 (from the United States) or (306) 653-2300
  http://www.sasktourism.com
- Alabama Shakespeare Festival
  http://www.mainstreetusa.com/

- Kentucky Shakespeare Festival
  http://www.kyshakes.org/
- Utah Shakespeare Festival, Southern Utah University,
  Cedar City, UT 84720; (435) 586-7878
  http://www.bard.org/

A SAMPLING OF RENFAIRES

- Arizona Renaissance Festival, 12601 East Highway 60,
  Apache Junction, AZ 85219; (520) 463-2600
- California Renaissance Pleasure Faires (Northern and
  Southern), P. O. Box B, Novato, CA 94948; (415) 892-0937
  or 800-52- FAIRE
  http://www.recfaie.com or http://www. renfair.com
- Georgia Renaissance Festival, P. O. Box 986, Fairburn, GA
  30213; (770) 964-8575
- Kansas City Renaissance Festival. 207 Westport Road, Suite
  206, Kansas City, MO 64111; (816) 561-8005
- King Richard's Faire, 2925 Dean Parkway, Suite 808, Minnea-
  polis, MN 55416; (612) 922-0777 or (508) 866-5391
- The Maryland Renaissance Festival, International Renaissance
  Festivals Ltd., P. O. Box 315, Crownsville, MD 21032;
  800-296-7304
- Michigan Renaissance Festival, 120 South Saginaw,
  Holly, MI 48442; 800-601-4848

- Minnesota Renaissance Faire, 1244 South Canterbury Road, Shakopee, MN 55379; 800-966-8215 or (612) 445-7361
- New York Renaissance Faire, P. O. Box 844, Tuxedo, NY 10987; (914) 351-5171 or 800-52-FAIRE
- Ohio Renaissance Festival, P. O. Box 68, Harveysburg, OH 45032-0068; (513) 897-7000
- Pennsylvania Renaissance Faire, P. O. Box 685, Cornwall, PA 17016; (717) 665-7021
  http://www.parenaissancefaire.com
- Texas Renaissance Festival, Route 2, Box 650, Plantersville, TX 77363; 800-458-3435
  http://www.texrenfest.com
- For Canada and other venues outside the United States, contact: International Renaissance Festivals, Limited, P. O. Box 486, Milton, Ontario, Canada.

selected bibliography

Anderson, Bonnie, and Judith Zinsser. *A History of Their Own,* Vol. I. New York: Harper & Row, 1988.

Bainton, Roland. *Women of the Reformation in France and England.* Minneapolis, MN: Augsburg Publishing House, 1971–1973.

———. *Women of the Reformation in Germany and Italy.* Augsburg Publishing House, 1971–1973.

———. *Women of the Reformation, from Spain to Scandinavia.* Augsburg Publishing House, 1971–1973.

Barstow, Anne L. *Witchcraze.* San Francisco: HarperSanFrancisco, 1995.

Berdes, Jane. *Women Musicians of Venice: Musical Foundations, 1525–1855.* New York: Oxford University Press, 1993.

Borzello, Frances. *Seeing Ourselves: Self Portraits by Women Artists.* New York: Abrams, 1998.

Boulding, Elise. *The Underside of History.* Newbury Park, CA: Sage Publications, 1992.

Buford, E. J. *London, the Synfulle Citie.* London: Robert Hale Ltd., 1990.

Chadwick, Whitney. *Women, Art and Society.* New York: Thames & Hudson, 1990.

Clark, Alice. *The Working Life of Women in the Seventeenth Century.* New York: Harcourt Brace, 1920.

Cook, Petronelle. *Queen Consorts of England.* New York: Facts on File, 1993.

Dekker, Rudolf, and Lotte van de Pol. *The Tradition of Female Transvestitism in Early Modern Europe.* New York: St. Martin's Press, 1989.

Feinberg, Leslie. *Transgender Warriors.* Boston: Beacon Press, 1996.

Fraser, Antonia. *Weaker Vessel.* New York: Vintage Books, 1994.

———. *The Wives of Henry VIII.* New York: Vintage Books, 1994.

———. *Cromwell: The Lord Protector.* New York: Knopf, 1973.

Greer, Germaine. *The Obstacle Race: The Fortunes of Women Painters and Their Work.* New York: Farrar Straus Giroux, 1979.

Haynes, Alan. *Sex in Elizabethan England.* Phoenix Mill, England: Sutton Publishing Ltd, 1997.

Henry, Sondra, and Emily Taitz. *Written out of History: Jewish Foremothers.* New York: Biblio Press, 1990.

Hogrefe, Pearl. *Tudor Women: Commoners and Queens.* Ammes, IA: Iowa State University Press, 1975.

King, Margaret. *Women of the Renaissance.* University of Chicago: Chicago Press, 1991.

King, Margaret, and Albert Rabil, eds. *Her Immaculate Hand,* Vol. 20. Wayland, MA: Medieval and Renaissance Texts & Studies, 1983.

Labarge, Margaret. *A Small Sound of the Trumpet.* Boston: Beacon Press, 1986.

León, Vicki. *Uppity Women of Medieval Times.* Berkeley, CA: Conari Press, 1997. For younger readers:

———. *Outrageous Women of Medieval Times.* New York: John Wiley & Sons, 1998.

———. *Outrageous Women of the Renaissance.* New York: John Wiley & Sons, 1999.

Marshall, Sherrin, ed. *Women in Reformation and Counter-Reformation Europe: Public and Private Worlds.* Bloomington, IN: Indiana University Press, 1989.

Maxwell, Robin. *The Secret Diary of Anne Boleyn.* New York: Arcade
Publishing, 1997.

Oglivie, Marilyn. *Women in Science: Antiquity Through the Nineteenth Century.*
Cambridge, MA: MIT Press, 1993.

Phillips, Patricia. *The Scientific Lady: A Social History of Women's Scientific Interests,
1520–1918.* St. New York: Martin's Press, 1990.

Picard, Liza. *Restoration London.* London: Weidenfeld & Nicolson, 1997.

Ridley, Jasper. *The Tudor Age.* New York: Overlook Press, 1990.

Ruggiero, Guido. *The Boundaries of Eros.* New York: Oxford University Press,
1985.

Sadie, Julie Ann, and Rhian Samuel. *The Norton/Grove Dictionary of Women
Composers.* New York: W. W. Norton, 1995.

Salgado, Gamini. *The Elizabethan Underworld.* Phoenix Mill, England: Sutton
Publishing Ltd, 1992.

Schama, Simon. *The Embarrassment of Riches.* New York: Knopf, 1987.

Uitz, Erika. *The Legend of Good Women.* Wakefield, RI: Moyer Bell, 1994.

Walker, Barbara. *Woman's Encyclopedia of Myths and Secrets.* San Francisco:
HarperSanFrancisco, 1996.

Wiesner, Merry. *Working Women in Renaissance Germany.* Piscataway, NJ:
Rutgers University Press, 1986.

Wilson, Derek. *The Tower.* New York: Charles Scribner's Sons, 1979.

Wilson, F. P. *The Plague in Shakespeare's London.* New York: Oxford University
Press, 1963.

INDEX OF UPPITY WOMEN

ca. *denotes circa*; a. *denotes active.*

Agnes Dürer (1471–ca. 1528), 248, 274

Agnes le Ismongere (a. 1346), 62

Agnes Louth (a. 1422), 173

Agnes Sadeler (a. 1386), 128

Agnes Sorel (1410–1450), 179

Albiera Albizzi (d. 1473), 117

Alessandra Bocchineri (ca. 1610–ca. 1650), 260

Alice Arden (a. 1550), 50

Alice Blague (a. 1599), 180

Alice Clark (a. 1629), 4, 128

Améliane de Glandèves (a. 1524), 24

Anna Bijns (1493–1575), 209

Anna Maria von Schurmann (1607–1678), 94, 170

Anna of Austria (a. 1655), 34

Anna Trapnel (a. 1650), 226

Anne Boleyn (ca. 1507–1536), 103, 239, 240, 241, 242

Anne Bracegirdle (a. 1660), 195

Anne Clifford (ca. 1590–1676), 66

Anne Cooke Bacon (ca. 1528–1610), 1, 261

Anne Hathaway (1556–1623), 268

Anne Lenclos, *see* Ninon de Lenclos

Anne Murray (a. 1647), 140

Anne of Cleves (1515–1557), 244

Anne of Denmark (1574–1619), 22

Anne Stagge (a. 1642), 129

Aphra Amis Behn (ca. 1640–1689), 136

Arcangela Tarabotti (1604–1652), 215

Argula von Grumbach (1492–ca. 1563), 230

Aubigny de Maupin (ca. 1673–1701), 8, 152

Barbara Strozzi (ca. 1619–ca. 1664), 16

Barbara Uttmann (1514–1575), 112

Bathsua Pell Makin (1612–ca. 1680), 170

bawdy baskets, 70

Beatrice Cenci (1577–1599), 76

Beatriz Galindo (1473–1535), 239

Benvenida Abravanel (ca. 1490–1560), 5, 56

"Bess O'Bedlam," 71

Bess Talbot of Hardwick (a. 1560), 5, 104

Bess Throckmorton (a. 1591), 266

Beth Kraus, (1559–1639), 75

Birgitta of Sweden (a. 1350), 216

"Bloody Mary" *see* Mary I of England

Bridget Bendish (a. 1670), 276

Cassandra Fedele (1475–1568), 1, 98
Catarina Cornaro (1454–1510), 32
Catarucia Zane (a. 1382), 88
Caterina de'Pazzi (1566–1607), 227
Catherine Deshayes de Monvoisin (a. 1650), 68
Catherine Howard (ca. 1521–1542), 103, 246
Catherine of Aragon (1485–1536), 238, 240, 242, 243, 254
Catherine Parr (1512–1548), 250
Catherine Sedley (1657–1717), 183
Cecilia Guardi (a. 1699), 284
Cecilia Vecelli (a. 1520), 283
Celia Fiennes (1662–1741), 156
Charlotte de la Trémoille (a. 1645), 174
Charlotte Guillard (ca. 1485–1557), 2, 168
Christian Davies (a. 1692), 160
Christina of Denmark (a. 1538), 241
Christine de Pizan (ca. 1364–1430), 121
Clarice di Durisio (ca.1350 –1410), 122
Cornelia Croon (a. 1670), 7, 155
Cristina Dandolo (a. 1382), 89

Damaris Page (a. 1600s), 96
Dark Lady, *see* Emilia Bassano, Mary Fitton
Dorothy Petty (a. 1695), 5, 101
Drutgin van Caster (a. 1500), 12

Edith Doddington (a. 1630), 100
Elena de Céspedes (ca. 1545–1588), 158
Elena Piscopia (ca. 1646–1684), 220
Elisabetta Sirani (1638–1665), 40
Elizabeth Alkin (a. 1647), 64
Elizabeth Allde (a. 1633), 51
Elizabeth Barry (a. 1660), 195
Elizabeth Barton (ca. 1506–1534), 240
Elizabeth Cellier (a. 1634), 120
Elizabeth Cresswell (a. 1600s), 96
Elizabeth Heyssin (a. 1596), 124
Elizabeth Hooton (a.1670), 214
Elizabeth Kraus, *see* Beth Kraus
Elizabeth of York (1466–1503), 247
Elizabeth I of England, (1528–1603), 71, 105, 180, 237, 239, 243, 251, 261, 266
Emilia Bassano (a. 1592), 269
Ersilia Santa Croce (a. 1563), 76
Eulalia Sagarra (a.1440), 5, 111

Francesca Caccini (1587–ca. 1638), 36
Frances Howard (a. 1613), 78
Frances Stelecrag (a. 1556), 30
Franchesina Sorenzo (a. 1341), 102
Francisca de Lebrija (a.1480), 239
Francisca Hernández (a. 1525), 218

Gesche Heimb (a. 1643), 52

Ginevra Nogarola (a. 1440), 1, 232
Giovanna Albizzi (1400?), 117
Giovanna Cenami Arnolfini (a. 1434), 273
Gracia Mendes (ca. 1510–1569), 57

Hendrickje Stoffels (a. 1650), 272, 288
Henrietta–Maria (1609–1666), 192, 280
Hester Davenport (a. 1661), 194
Hester Ogden (a. 1660), 2, 190
Hester Shaw (a. 1634), 120
Holy Maid of Kent, *see* Elizabeth Barton

Ilona Szilagy (a. 1462), 264
Inés de Castro (a. 1347), 270
Isabel Berkeley (a. 1424), 114
Isabel la Católica (1451–1504), 239
Isabella Clara Eugenia (a.1590), 285
Isabella Geelvinck (a. 1650), 7, 138
Isabelle Warwicke (a. 1572), 122
Isotta Nogarola (1418–1466), 1, 232

Jadwiga of Poland (1373–1399), 58
Jadwige Gnoinskiej (a. 1567), 206
Jane Grey (1537–1554), 252
Jane Sharp (a. 1634), 120
Jane Shore (ca. 1447–1527), 61
Jane Whorwood (a. 1647), 47
Jeanne d'Albret (1528–1572), 72

Jehanne de Marnef (a. 1545), 29
Joan Dant (1631–1715), 5, 162
Joan Hunt (a. 1365), 125
Joan of Navarre (ca. 1370–1437), 3, 42
Joan Waste (a. 1557), 255
Johanna Koorton Blok (a. 1675), 39
Juana de la Cruz (a. 1509), 228
Judith Johannes (a. mid–1600s), 18
Judith Leyster (1609–ca. 1668), 20
Judith Philips (a. 1595), 80
Judith Shakespeare (a. 1600), 268
Julia Lombardo (a. 1530), 118

Karyssa Under Helmslegern (a. 1450), 5, 108
Katharine Elliot (a. 1600s), 95
Katherina Amlingyn (a. 1595), 109
Katherine Boyle, *see* Sister Ranelagh
Katherine Grey (a. 1553), 253
Kathy Krapp Melanchthon (a. 1530), 54
Katie von Bora (1499–1550), 5, 258
Kristina of Sweden (1626–1689), 148

La Branlaire (a. 1650), 129
La Grosse Margot (a. 1440), 126
Laura Cereta (1469–1499), 1, 186
La Voisin, *see* Catherine Deshayes de Monvoisin

Leonora de Toledo (a. 1530), 56

Leonor López de Córdoba (a. 1406), 130

Long Meg (a. early 1500s?), 8, 146

Louise of Savoy (a. 1529), 172

Lucrezia Borgia (1480–1519), 68, 210

Lucrezia Buti (a. 1460), 293

Lucrezia Petroni (a. 1598), 76

Luisa Roldán (1656–1704), 26

Lydwina of Schiedam (a. 1400), 18

Macée Trepperel (a. 1520), 28

Madalena dal Violin (a. 1500s?), 198

Maddalena Casulana (ca. 1540–1583), 16

Maddalena Ruíz (a. late 1500s), 285

Madge Shelton (a. 1527), 241

Madge Tyler (a. 1578), 103

Mancini sisters (a. 1679), 69

Margaret Baynham (a. 1534), 106

Margaret Beaufort (1443 –1509), 236

Margaret Fell (1614–ca. 1698), 5, 212

Margaret Lucas Cavendish (1625–1673), 94, 192

Margaret of Austria (1480–1530), 172

Margarita from the Mendicanti (a. 1500s?), 199

Margarita of Venice (a. 1395), 83

Margherita Caccini (a. 1640), 38

Mariana Alcoforado (1640–1723), 200

Marie de'Medici (1573–1642), 36, 46

Marie le Jars de Gourney (1565–1645), 2, 92

Marie Scholtus (a. mid–1600s), 18

Marina Gamba (a. 1597), 262

Maritgen Jens (a. 1600s), 150

Mary d'Oignies (d. 1213), 117

Marye Baugaurd (a. 1550), 169

Mary Fitton (a. 1590), 269

Mary of Hungary (1505–1558), 144

Mary I of England, (1516–1558), 239, 253, 254

Mary, Queen of Scots (1542–1587), 19

Mary Seymour (1548–ca.1560), 251

Matilda Hereward (a. 1301), 86

Meg Blague (a. 1666), 110

Miss Hobart (a. mid–1600s), 188

Mother Shipton, *see* Ursula Shipton

Mrs. Diogo Afonso (a. 1432), 14

Mrs. Jane Doe (a. 1443), 182

Nell Gwynn (ca. 1650–1687), 166

Ninon de Lenclos (1616–1706), 204

Novella Andrea (a. late 1300s), 121

Olimpia Morata (1526–1555), 1,
142, 224
Oliva Sabuco de Nantes Barrera (a.
1587), 189
Oliva the Goldsmith (a. 1330), 12
Olympia Maidalchini (a. 1650), 55

"Parliament Joan," *see* Elizabeth Alkin
Perette of Rouen (a. 1400), 60
Perreta Betonne (a. 1407), 122
Priss Fotheringham (a. mid–1600s),
96
Prudenza da Contralto (a.
mid–1500s), 198

Rebecca Cooper (a. 1650), 31
Rebecca Marshall (a. 1670), 195
Renée of France (1510–1575), 224
Rosa Vanozza (1442–1518), 210
Roxelana (a. mid–1500s), 176, 194

Sarel Gutman (a. 1619), 164
Saskia van Ulenborch (ca.
1612–1642), 272, 288
Settimia Caccini (1591–ca. 1661), 36
"Sherriff Anne Clifford," *see* Anne
Clifford
Simonetta Cattanei Vespucci
(ca. 1455–1476), 117
Sister Ranelagh (1614–1691), 286
Sister Sara of Ferrara (a. 1432), 202
Sophia of Russia (a. 1682), 290

Spanish witch kids (a. 1611), 44
Susanna Hornebolt (ca. 1505–ca.
1548), 248
Susanna Shakespeare (a. 1600), 268
Suzanne Erker (a. 1560), 13

Tarquinia Molza (a. 1570), 16
Teresa of Ávila (1515–1582), 222
Thomasine Bonaventura Barnaby
Gall Percival (a. 1470), 84
Trijn Jurriaens (a. 1679), 134
Trijntje Simon (a. 1500s?), 8, 133

Ursula Fladin (a. 1581), 3, 10
Ursula Shipton (a. 1535), 256

Veronica Franco (a. 1570), 184
Violante do Céu (a. 1650), 203
Virginia Galilei (ca. 1598–1634),
262

Wibrandis Rosenblatt (1504–1564),
208
Widowe Lovejoye (a. 1639), 116
Widow Trepperel (a. 1500), 28

Yolande Bonhomme (a. 1557), 28

Zabetta of the Incurabili (a. early
1500s?), 198
Zoe Palaiologina (ca. 1444–1503),
278

VICKI LEÓN

The author of twenty–six books, including *Uppity Women of Ancient Times* and *Uppity Women of Medieval Times,* Vicki León also delights in giving workshops and speeches on the unsung women of history. She lives in southwest Washington.

CONARI PRESS, established in 1987, publishes books on topics ranging from psychology, spirituality, and women's history to sexuality, parenting, and personal growth. Our main goal is to publish quality books that will make a difference in people's lives—both how we feel about ourselves and how we relate to one another.

Our readers are our most important resource, and we value your input, suggestions, and ideas. We'd love to hear from you—after all, we are publishing books for you!

To request our latest book catalog, or to be added to our mailing list, please contact:

CONARI PRESS
2550 Ninth Street, Suite 101
Berkeley, California 94710-2551
800–685–9595   510-649-7175

fax: 510-649-7190   e-mail: Conaripub@aol.com
http://www.readersNdex.com/conari/